Prevention RD's
Everyday Healthy Cooking

100 Light and Delicious Recipes to Promote Energy, Weight Loss, and Well-Being

Nicole Morrissey
Founder of *Prevention RD*
Registered Dietitian and Diabetes Educator

Skyhorse Publishing

Copyright © 2013 by Nicole Morrissey

Photographs Copyright © by Nicole Morrissey

Skyhorse Publishing books may be purchased in bulk at special discounts for sales promotion, corporate gifts, fund-raising, or educational purposes. Special editions can also be created to specifications. For details, contact the Special Sales Department, Skyhorse Publishing, 307 West 36th Street, 11th Floor, New York, NY 10018 or info@skyhorsepublishing.com.

Skyhorse® and Skyhorse Publishing® are registered trademarks of Skyhorse Publishing, Inc.®, a Delaware corporation.

Visit our website at www.skyhorsepublishing.com.

10 9 8 7 6 5 4 3 2 1

Library of Congress Cataloging-in-Publication Data is available on file.

ISBN: 978-1-62087-689-3

Printed in India

Contents

Acknowledgments

I've always loved to write, and I've always LOVED food—so to see two of my loves marry into this cookbook is a dream come true. Sometimes in life, you're lucky enough to have personal cheerleaders who root for your every move. I was blessed enough to have a personal cheerleader who, sadly, was taken early from this Earth after a very short battle with Amyotrophic lateral sclerosis (ALS). Shirley Roberts was a strong, selfless, and independent woman. When I started my blog in 2009, she quickly became a loyal reader. "Nik, I really think you should write a cookbook," she would say. I would smile and brush off her encouragement with a small roll of my eyes—a very bad habit of mine.

Today, I know Shirley is smiling down on me and thinking, "I told you so." And, she was right. To one of my greatest personal cheerleaders: Thank you for believing in what I could accomplish when I had no clue.

When I was approached about writing a cookbook based on my blog, I was flattered and also completely floored by the inquiry. Sometimes you never know what impact you have through words, especially when you send your thoughts into the depths of the World Wide Web with very little knowledge as to who may be reading. Yet, my blog has enriched my life in every way. The people who come to my corner of the web have helped me grow through their love, appreciation, and wisdom.

To my readers: Thank you—for reading, for cooking, and for eating to good health. May you have a personal cheerleader and know that you are one for me.

Introduction

It wasn't until I started losing weight at age fourteen that I gave consideration to nutrition for the first time. Having been overweight my whole life, I knew at that point—like it, love it, or hate it—I would have to be nutrition-savvy to gain control over the scale . . . and my life.

I tried many diets—Atkins, South Beach, Weight Watchers, you name it. By the time I was seventeen, I was so burned out on calorie counting and food journaling, but I had taken off weight through old-fashioned calorie control and exercise. I felt great and was heading off to college to study nutrition and become a registered dietitian (RD). I always felt sorry for my peers who didn't know what they wanted to be "when they grew up." Since high school, I knew I wanted to be a dietitian, and that has never changed.

College flew by, as did graduate school. I passed my RD exam and was high on life, especially with my wedding just months away in the spring of 2009. However, I was in search of my first job as a dietitian in the worst economic downturn since the Great Depression, and I was having no luck. I was bored, sitting at home, feeling hopeless but yet so excited to share with the world all that I had learned about nutrition. I decided to start a blog.

My blog didn't start as a recipe blog because . . . I didn't really cook. I would write about interesting nutrition opinion pieces or news articles that focused on controversial nutrition topics, and I would weigh in online. It was fun, but it wasn't my passion.

I wish I could pinpoint when the transition occurred, but before I knew it, I had morphed into this quintessential wife who planned meals, prepared grocery lists, and put a hot, home-cooked meal on the table each night for my husband—a husband who would be happiest with a steady diet of pizza and anything buffalo wing-y. So, my culinary journey began. What would he eat? How could I appease him while maintaining my weight-loss? What fits into the busy lives of a dual career couple?

When people ask me what "my specialty" is, I don't really have a good answer. What I do is make foods that anyone and everyone loves to eat . . . and I make them healthier. I'm not vegetarian, vegan, or gluten-free, but I dabble in them all. I believe in balance and omitting no food from my diet. My approach to nutrition is one that is maintainable and *enjoyable*. If you don't love what you're eating, why would you continue to eat the same tomorrow, much less forever?

I continue to struggle with my weight and probably always will. The good news is I've found a perfect balance of what I love and what I need while living a life that is balanced and strong. So much of finding that balance started with eating well, moving more, and focusing on health over weight. I hope this cookbook and my blog represent that and inspire you to find your balance in pursuit of health and happiness.

The recipes I make are calorie-controlled, with most recipes falling between 350 and 500 calories per serving. I use healthier alternatives for ingredients without sacrificing the integrity of the final product. While many of the recipes I post are appropriate for disease management (diabetes, hypertension, etc.), I focus more on the prevention of disease through promoting an overall balanced diet. Hence, *Prevention RD*.

Thanks for reading. Be well!

Nicole Morrissey

Look for These Icons

You will see the icons below on various recipes included in this collection. They will indicate whether a recipe is vegetarian or vegan, dairy-free or gluten-free. You can use these icons to quickly spot meals that are perfect for diabetics or that require little preparation.

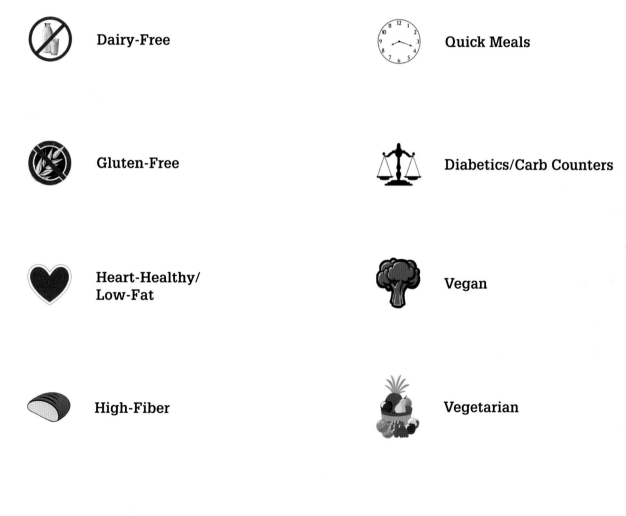

Dairy-Free

Gluten-Free

**Heart-Healthy/
Low-Fat**

High-Fiber

Quick Meals

Diabetics/Carb Counters

Vegan

Vegetarian

Noshing

Smashed Edamame, Avocado, and Ricotta Dip

Pepperoni Pizza Puffs

Buffalo Wing Hummus

Fresh Grilled Salsa

Crispy Baked Egg rolls

Cheesy Baked Artichoke Dip

Oven-Fried Pickles

Wonton Chicken Tacos

Baked Mozzarella Sticks

Chipotle Shrimp
with Avocado Dipping Sauce

White Wine and Garlic
Steamed Mussels

Smashed Edamame, Avocado, and Ricotta Bean Dip

1 (15-oz.) can cannellini beans, drained
   and rinsed
1 avocado
½ cup edamame, shelled
1 cup low-fat ricotta

½ cup basil, loosely packed
¼ cup (1 oz.) Parmesan cheese, grated
   or finely shredded
Juice of ½ lemon
½ teaspoon salt

Directions:

Combine all ingredients in a food processor or blender, and puree until smooth, scraping down the sides as needed.

Yield:

3½ cups (14 servings, ¼ cup each)

Nutrition Information (per serving):

80 calories; 3.6 g fat; 6 mg cholesterol; 198 mg sodium;
7.2 g carbohydrate; 2.6 g fiber; 4.2 g protein

Nutrition Note:

This dip packs tons of flavor and nutrition. I started with a bean and avocado base and added some of my other favorites: ricotta, basil, cheese, and lemon. Full of healthful fat and fiber, this is a colorful starter that's sure to please.

Pepperoni Pizza Puffs

¾ cup flour

¼ teaspoon baking powder

¼ teaspoon salt

½ teaspoon dried oregano

¾ cup fat-free milk

1 egg, lightly beaten

4 oz. (1 cup) part-skim mozzarella cheese, shredded

34 slices turkey pepperoni, quartered

½ cup pizza sauce (homemade or store-bought)

2 tablespoons fresh basil, thinly sliced

Directions:

Preheat oven to 375°F. Grease a 24-cup mini-muffin pan.

In a large bowl, whisk together flour, baking powder, salt, and oregano; whisk in milk and egg. Stir in mozzarella and pepperoni; let stand 10 minutes.

Stir batter, and divide among mini-muffin cups. Bake until puffed and golden, 20–25 minutes.

Warm pizza sauce, then stir in 1 tablespoon basil. Sprinkle puffs with remaining 1 tablespoon basil. Serve puffs with pizza sauce for dipping.

Yield:

24 pizza puffs

Nutrition Information (per pizza puff):

38 calories; 1.4 g fat; 14 mg cholesterol; 123 mg sodium; 3.5 g carbohydrate; 0.1 g fiber; 3.0 g protein

Fun Fact:

These are the ultimate kid food and are perfect for casual get-togethers and game days. Choose a pizza sauce you love for dunking . . . the sauce is what makes these truly pizza-like!

Buffalo Wing Hummus

2 cans chickpeas, drained and rinsed
2–3 cloves garlic
¼ cup tahini
¼ cup fresh lemon juice

1½ teaspoons paprika
3 tablespoons calorie-free wing sauce
2 tablespoons cayenne hot sauce
1 tablespoon distilled white vinegar
½ teaspoon kosher salt

Directions:

Put chickpeas, garlic, tahini, lemon juice, paprika, wing sauce, hot sauce, vinegar, and salt in a food processor. Puree until smooth and creamy.

Yield:

12 servings (¼ cup each)

Nutrition Information (per serving):

99 calories; 3.4 g fat; 0 mg cholesterol; 231 mg sodium; 11.8 g carbohydrate; 4.2 g fiber; 4.6 g protein

Nutrition Note:

As much as I love buffalo wing sauce, it's important to use it in moderation. Even though calorie-free versions are readily available, they are packed with sodium. Using the buffalo wing sauce in this recipe aims at getting the flavor while keeping sodium levels in check and packing in both nutrition and great taste. Serve this with celery to make it a low-calorie snack that's high in fiber.

Fresh Grilled Salsa

2 teaspoons extra virgin olive oil, to coat
6 large tomatoes
1–3 jalapeños (1 for mild, 2 for medium,
   3 for hot)

1 onion, peeled and quartered
½ head of garlic, unpeeled
1 bunch cilantro
1 teaspoon salt
Juice of ½ lime

Directions:

Pre-heat grill to medium heat. Coat tomatoes, jalapeños, onion, and garlic in olive oil.

Grill vegetables until they are charred but not falling apart. Place all ingredients (including cilantro, salt, and lime juice) in a blender, and blend until smooth.

Yield:

Approximately 6 cups (24 servings, ¼ cup each)

Nutrition Information (per ¼ cup):

17 calories; 0.45 g fat; 0 mg cholesterol; 97 mg sodium; 2.8 g carbohydrate; 0.7 g fiber; 0.6 g protein

Fun Fact:

I adapted this recipe from *Biz of My Bizzy Kitchen,* one of my favorite blogs. Over the years, I think this is the recipe I'm best known for among my social circle—I take it everywhere there's a crowd. This recipe takes 10 minutes to make and keeps well for 5 days in the refrigerator. This recipe can be adapted to be mild and spicy and can include any number of ingredients. I love to add a lot of garlic and plenty of jalapeño and onion.

Crispy Baked Egg Rolls

14 oz. coleslaw mix (cabbage and carrots)
1 tablespoon olive oil
2 garlic cloves, minced
Pinch of ground ginger

1 tablespoon low-sodium soy sauce
12 egg roll wrappers
1 tablespoon flour plus 1½ tablespoons water
Cooking spray

Shopping Tip:

Large grocery retailers carry wonton and egg roll wrappers in the produce section near the tofu. These low-calorie wrappers make for fun appetizers in cute sizes and shapes.

Directions:

Preheat oven to 425°F. Spray a baking sheet with cooking spray, and set aside.

In a large skillet, heat olive oil over medium heat. Once hot, add coleslaw mix and garlic. Sauté 4–5 minutes or until cabbage is soft but not soggy. Add ginger and soy sauce; stir to combine. Remove from heat, and set aside to cool briefly.

In a small dish, whisk together flour and water to form a thin paste.

Spoon 3 tablespoons cabbage mixture into the middle of each of 12 egg roll wrappers. Working at a diagonal, use a finger to smear some of the flour-water paste on each of three corners of the wrapper. Roll from the un-smeared side, and seal each wrapper into a log. Place each egg roll onto the baking sheet.

Bake egg rolls for 12–14 minutes or until they begin to brown. For added crispiness, put egg rolls in the broiler for 1–2 minutes, checking them every 20–30 seconds. Remove, and allow to cool for several minutes.

Yield:

6 servings (2 egg rolls each)

Nutrition Information (per serving):

160 calories; 2.3 g fat; 7 mg cholesterol; 390 mg sodium; 28.5 g carbohydrate; 2.3 g fiber; 5.8 g protein

Cheesy Baked Artichoke Dip

½ cup (2 oz.) plus 2 teaspoons grated
   Parmesan cheese, divided
⅓ cup low-fat mayonnaise
⅓ cup 0% plain Greek yogurt
¼ teaspoon ground black pepper
½ teaspoon garlic powder

¼ teaspoon onion powder
2 (14-oz.) cans artichoke hearts packed in
   water, drained, and chopped into
   ¼-inch pieces
½ cup (2 oz.) 2% Italian cheese blend,
   shredded

Directions:

Preheat oven to 375°F.

Combine Parmesan cheese, mayonnaise, yogurt, and spices in medium-sized bowl to blend. Stir in chopped artichoke hearts. Transfer mixture to casserole dish.

Sprinkle dip with remaining 2 teaspoons grated Parmesan cheese and Italian cheese blend. Bake dip until heated through, about 25–30 minutes. To brown the top, broil at 500°F until cheese bubbles and browns, about 2–3 minutes.

Serve warm with toasted baguette slices.

Yield:

10 (¼ cup per serving)

Nutrition Information (per ¼ cup):

89 calories; 4.5 g fat; 10 mg cholesterol; 259 mg sodium;
6.2 g carbohydrate; 1.2 g fiber; 5.9 g protein

Nutrition Note:

When a recipe calls for mayonnaise, I not only opt for a low-fat version, but I also substitute out half of the mayonnaise for plain Greek yogurt. By doing so, I decrease the fat content and calories while increasing the nutrition. Plain Greek yogurt always is stocked in my refrigerator for breakfast, snacks, and recipes.

Oven-Fried Pickles

1 20-oz. jar Claussen Kosher dill pickle slices
   (about 16 slices)
2 eggs
⅓ cup flour
1 tablespoon Worcestershire sauce

1 teaspoon hot sauce
1 teaspoon garlic powder
1 teaspoon Cajun seasoning
1 teaspoon pepper
1½ cups panko bread crumbs

Directions:

Turn oven broiler on to 450°F.

In a medium-sized bowl, whisk together eggs and flour. Add Worcestershire, hot sauce, garlic powder, Cajun seasoning, and pepper to egg mixture. Mix well.

Place panko bread crumbs in a shallow dish. Dunk each pickle slice into egg mixture, then dredge it in panko bread crumbs.

Place coated pickles on a baking sheet that's been coated with nonstick cooking spray. Place pan in middle rack of oven. Broil about 2–3 minutes on each side until golden brown, adding time if needed.

Yield:

4 servings (4 pickles each)

Nutrition Information (per 4 pickles):

171 calories; 2.8 g fat; 107 mg cholesterol; 1028 mg sodium; 30 g carbohydrate; 0.3 g fiber; 7 g protein

Fun Fact:

Fried pickles are a staple in the South. When my husband and I moved to Tulsa, it was difficult to find a restaurant that didn't have fried pickles on the menu. Some versions use spears versus chips, but I like to find thick pickle chips for this recipe. This version brings all the crunch of fried pickles with none of the guilt!

Wonton Chicken Tacos

12 square wonton wrappers
3 oz. cooked chicken, shredded
¼ cup 2% Mexican-blend cheese, shredded

¼ cup lettuce, shredded
1 tablespoon red onion, finely diced
2 tablespoons tomato, finely diced

Directions:

Preheat oven to 400°F.

Cook and shred chicken (leftover chicken is perfect).

In a mini-muffin tin, gently press a wonton wrapper into each of the 12 wells. Distribute chicken and cheese evenly among the 12 wells. Bake for 7–9 minutes, until wonton edges are golden brown.

Top with lettuce, onion, and tomato. Serve immediately.

Yield:

12 wonton tacos

Nutrition Information (per wonton):

32 calories; 0.6 g fat; 6 mg cholesterol; 60 mg sodium; 3.6 g carbohydrate; 0.16 g fiber; 2.9 g protein

Cook's Comment:

People go crazy for bite-sized finger foods—it's a fact! Between the fun shapes and angles of these tacos and the ability to add, or subtract, any and every ingredient, these are perfect for a crowd. They come together in a few short minutes, and you can fill them with anything.

Baked Mozzarella Sticks

6 part-skim mozzarella cheese sticks

12 egg roll wrappers

Canola or olive oil cooking spray

½ cup marinara sauce of choice

Directions:

Preheat oven to 400°F.

Cut cheese sticks in half lengthwise so they are about 2½ inches long.

Lay egg roll wrapper at a diagonal, put one piece of cheese at the very corner, and begin to roll into a log. At the mid-point of the wrapper, fold in each of the sides, and continue rolling. Seal off the egg roll wrapper with a smear of water along the edges, and rub to moisten and seal.

Arrange mozzarella sticks on a parchment-lined baking sheet, and spray lightly with olive oil. Bake for 12–15 minutes or until lightly browned.

Yield:

12 servings (1 mozzarella stick each)

Nutrition Information (per serving):

90 calories; 1.3 g fat; 8 mg cholesterol; 251 mg sodium; 12.3 g carbohydrate; 0.3 g fiber; 6.4 g protein

Cook's Comment:

Spraying with olive oil helps to make food golden and crisp. If you haven't invested in an oil spritzer, it's time to do so. A few pumps, and you're off. You'll never buy cooking spray again, and all of your baked goods will be perfectly browned.

Chipotle Shrimp with Avocado Dipping Sauce

1 lb large shrimp (about 24), peeled
   and deveined
1 tablespoon cumin
1 tablespoon chili powder
Pinch of cayenne

Dipping Sauce:
1 avocado
¼ cup nonfat Greek yogurt
1 teaspoon cumin
½ teaspoon chili powder
Juice of ¼ lime
¼ teaspoon salt

Cook's Comment:

Cayenne pepper is spicy—use it with caution if you prefer things mild. These spicy shrimp are a nice change from the ever-popular shrimp cocktail. The avocado dipping sauce cools the palate with each bite.

Directions:

Preheat oven to 450°F. Line a baking sheet with tinfoil, and mist with olive oil or cooking spray.

Toss shrimp with spices, and arrange on the baking sheet. Bake 6–7 minutes.

Meanwhile, mash avocado with the backside of a fork, and mix in remaining ingredients for the dipping sauce. Serve immediately.

Yield:

6 servings (4 shrimp with 3 tablespoons dipping sauce)

Nutrition Information (per serving):

138 calories; 6.2 g fat; 100 mg cholesterol; 208 mg sodium; 4.3 g carbohydrate; 2.5 g fiber; 17 g protein

White Wine and Garlic Steamed Mussels

3 lbs mussels, fresh or frozen
½ cup white wine
1 cup low-sodium chicken broth

2 tablespoons unsalted butter
4 cloves garlic, minced

Directions:

Discard any opened mussels. Scrub mussels to remove dirt and sand.

In a large pot, combine wine, broth, butter, and garlic; bring to a boil over medium-high heat. Put mussels into pot, and cover with lid. Steam 5–7 minutes or until mussels open. Serve immediately.

Yield:

5 appetizer servings (about 6 mussels each)

Nutrition Information (per serving):

126 calories; 4.0 g fat; 46 mg cholesterol; 239 mg sodium; 6.4 g carbohydrate; 0.4 g fiber; 13.8 g protein

Fun Fact:

Mussels are best when purchased alive… like lobsters. Don't be afraid! Keep them on ice, and purchase them no more than 24 hours before you plan to serve them. If a mussel is opened before cooking, discard it, because it has died. It's typical to have several dead mussels in a 3- to 5-lb bag. The actual preparation of mussels could not be any easier, and they are a real treat without the high price tag of other seafood fare. Try something new!

Eat More of These

Lightened-Up Caesar Salad

Roasted Asparagus with Balsamic Tomatoes

Mediterranean Salmon Salad
with Vinaigrette

Baked Mushrooms with Herbed
Bread Crumb Topping

Buttermilk Whipped Cauliflower
Mashed Potatoes

Light Buttermilk Ranch Dressing

Roasted Blue Cheese Brussels Sprouts

Mayo-Free Chicken Salad

Pesto Mashed Potatoes in a Portobello Cap

Berry Spinach Salad with Blueberry Vinaigrette

Roasted Winter Squash with Herbed Sugar Glaze

Paprika Oven Fries

Watermelon and Arugula Salad

Creamy Avocado Potato Salad

Broccoli with Light Cheese Sauce

Arugula Salad
with Grilled Peaches and Honey Goat Cheese Dressing

Lightened-Up Caesar Salad

Salad Dressing:

½ cup light mayonnaise

2 tablespoons red wine vinegar

2 teaspoons Dijon mustard

2 teaspoons white wine or white
   balsamic vinegar

1 teaspoon Worcestershire sauce

1 teaspoon anchovy paste

1 clove garlic, minced

⅛ teaspoon ground red pepper

Croutons:

6 oz. miniature multi-grain or whole-grain loaf, cubed

1 tablespoon olive oil

½ teaspoon garlic powder

Salad:

2 large heads Romaine, washed, dried, and ripped into bite-sized pieces

½ cup (2 oz.) Parmesan cheese, shredded

Directions:

Whisk salad dressing ingredients together in a small bowl. If time permits, cover and chill for at least 1 hour for flavors to blend.

Preheat oven to 350°F. Cube bread, and toss with olive oil. Arrange cubes on a baking sheet lined with tinfoil, and sprinkle with garlic salt. Bake for 20–25 minutes or until bread cubes are golden.

Place lettuce and croutons in a large bowl. Add dressing, and toss to coat thoroughly. Sprinkle with cheese, and serve.

Yield:

5 salad entrée portions (about 3 cups each)

Nutrition Information (per serving):

258 calories; 16.0 g fat; 18 g cholesterol; 654 mg sodium;

27.4 g carbohydrate; 7.0 g fiber; 11.2 g protein

Nutrition Note:

This is a generous portion of Caesar salad with croutons and cheese—there's no beating it! Add some grilled shrimp or chicken to make this a heavier meal that is still nutritious. It's difficult to go back to a calorie-packed salad after tasting this lightened-up version!

Roasted Asparagus with Balsamic Tomatoes

1 lb asparagus

4 teaspoons olive oil, divided

10 oz. cherry tomatoes

2 tablespoons balsamic vinegar

¼ teaspoon salt and pepper, to taste

Directions:

Preheat oven to 350°F.

Line a baking sheet with tinfoil, and spray with nonstick cooking spray.

Wash asparagus, break off tough end, and discard. Lay asparagus on the baking sheet, and drizzle with 3 teaspoons olive oil. Season with salt and pepper; roast 12–14 minutes or until tender.

Meanwhile, heat remaining teaspoon olive oil in a small pan over medium-high heat. Add tomatoes, and season with salt and pepper. Cook tomatoes 5 minutes, stirring occasionally. Add balsamic vinegar to the pan, and continue cooking an additional 5–6 minutes.

Serve tomatoes over asparagus.

Yield:

4 servings (about 5–6 stalks each)

Nutrition Information (per serving):

70 calories; 4.8 g fat; 0 mg cholesterol; 151 mg sodium; 6 g carbohydrate; 2.3 g fiber; 1.8 g protein

Cook's Comment:

I love asparagus, but my absolute favorite way to prepare it is to roast it. While I typically default to olive oil, salt, and pepper, this take on roasted asparagus includes cherry tomatoes that have been simmered in balsamic vinegar. The cherries slowly will burst in their skins and absorb all of the flavors. The red against the green makes for one stunning side!

Mediterranean Salmon Salad with Vinaigrette

Dressing:
⅓ cup olive oil
⅓ cup red wine vinegar
1¼ teaspoons dried oregano
1¼ teaspoons dried basil
1¼ teaspoons garlic powder
1 teaspoon onion powder
½ teaspoon salt
½ teaspoon pepper
1 teaspoon Dijon mustard

Salad:
¾-lb salmon filet
⅛ teaspoon salt
Pinch of black pepper
¼ teaspoon dried oregano
1 cup dried orzo
¼ cup kalamata olives, halved
1 red bell pepper, chopped
½ red onion, chopped
½ cup (2 oz.) crumbled feta cheese
1 (14-oz.) can artichoke hearts, quartered
5 cups spring mix, lightly packed
Dressing

Cook's Comment:

Many vinaigrettes use a 2-to-1 ratio of oil-to-vinegar. Using a 1-to-1 ratio and adding more oil, if needed, helps to keep the calories and fat content in check. This vinaigrette has so many added flavors that a little bit goes a long way. This salad is full of different flavors that work beautifully together. This salad is memorable, for sure

Directions:

Whisk all dressing ingredients together; set aside.

Preheat oven to 425°F.

Place salmon on a baking sheet lined with tinfoil and sprayed with olive oil. Sprinkle salmon with salt, pepper, and oregano. Bake 10-15 minutes or until no longer opaque.

Meanwhile, bring 1 quart water to a rolling boil in a medium-sized pot. Add orzo, and cook for 7–9 minutes until al dente. Drain pasta, and place in a deep casserole dish. Pour ¼ cup of dressing over pasta, and gently toss. To orzo, add olives, red bell peppers, red onions, feta, artichoke hearts, spring mix lettuce, and remaining dressing. Toss to gently combine all ingredients.

Once salmon is cooked, flake salmon using two forks. Top salad with flaked salmon.

Yield:

5 servings (1 cup lettuce with approximately 1 cup orzo-vegetable mix)

Nutrition Information (per serving):

500 calories; 24.6 g fat; 48 mg cholesterol; 614 mg sodium;
45 g carbohydrate; 5.4 g fiber; 25 g protein

Baked Mushrooms with Herbed Bread Crumb Topping

1 lb mushrooms, cleaned with stems removed
2 tablespoons unsalted butter, melted
¼ cup bread crumbs

1–2 tablespoons fresh herbs, minced (rosemary, sage, thyme)
¼ teaspoon salt and pepper, to taste

Directions:

Preheat oven to 350°F.

Spray casserole dish with cooking spray, and arrange mushrooms with the cap upside down.

Combine melted butter and bread crumbs in a small dish. Sprinkle over mushrooms, getting much of topping into wells where stems were removed. Sprinkle with herbs.

Bake 20 minutes, and serve immediately.

Yield:

5 servings (4–5 mushrooms each)

Nutrition Information (per serving):

83 calories; 4.8 g fat; 0 mg cholesterol; 151 mg sodium; 6.6 g carbohydrate; 1.4 g fiber; 3.8 g protein

Nutrition Note:

Fresh herbs are virtually calorie-free and are packed with flavor and antioxidants. Using fresh herbs can take a simple side dish and create flavors that will exceed your every expectation. Start an herb garden; buying fresh herbs as needed can become expensive!

Use gluten-free bread crumbs for a gluten-free meal!

Buttermilk Whipped Cauliflower Mashed Potatoes

4 medium-sized potatoes (about 1 lb), diced into large cubes

2½ cups cauliflower (about ½ large head)

⅓ cup low-fat buttermilk

1 tablespoon unsalted butter

2 oz. reduced-fat cream cheese

½ teaspoon salt

½ teaspoon pepper

Dried parsley, to taste

Directions:

Bring a large pot of water to boil. Add potatoes, and boil for 15–20 minutes, until fork-tender.

Add cauliflower, and continue to boil an additional 15–20 minutes.

Remove potatoes and cauliflower from water, and add remaining ingredients. Whip potatoes in a stand mixer fitted with the whisk attachment, or beat with a hand mixer until smooth and fluffy. Serve immediately.

Yield:

5 servings (1 cup each)

Nutrition Information (per serving):

142 calories; 4.8 g fat; 8 mg cholesterol; 308 mg sodium; 19.8 g carbohydrate; 3 g fiber; 4.8 g protein

Nutrition Note:

To cut calories, use cauliflower in place of potatoes. While I find no need to swap out all of the potatoes, swapping in cauliflower adds a fun taste and texture. People will never know these aren't the "real" deal!

Light Buttermilk Ranch Dressing

½ cup low-fat mayonnaise

1 cup fat-free Greek yogurt

2 teaspoons olive oil

1 cup low-fat buttermilk

3 tablespoons fresh chives, finely chopped

¼ cup fresh parsley, chopped

1 large clove garlic, minced

Juice of ½ lemon

½ teaspoon salt

½ teaspoon freshly ground black pepper

Directions:

In a blender or food processor, combine all ingredients, and puree until smooth. Taste and season with additional salt and pepper, if desired.

Store in an airtight container or a jar in the refrigerator.

Yield:

20 servings (2 tablespoons each)

Nutrition Information (per serving):

30 calories; 2 g fat; 3 mg cholesterol; 126 mg sodium; 1.7 g carbohydrate; 0 g fiber; 1.6 g protein

Nutrition Note:

Low-fat buttermilk is a favorite ingredient of mine. It is tart and perfect in so many recipes—in everything from salad dressing to muffins. It's also much more healthful than mayonnaise. I prefer my ranch dressing to have a strong buttermilk flavor; this recipe doubles up the buttermilk and consequently lowers the calories to fewer than half of even a low-fat ranch dressing variety you would find in stores.

Roasted Blue Cheese Brussels Sprouts

1 lb Brussels sprouts, halved

1 tablespoon olive oil

¼ teaspoon salt

¼ teaspoon pepper

2 oz. blue cheese, crumbled

Directions:

Preheat oven to 400°F.

Line a baking sheet with tinfoil or parchment, and mist with olive oil.

Toss together Brussels sprouts, olive oil, salt, and pepper. Arrange on the baking sheet in a single layer. Bake 20–25 minutes or until edges begin to brown.

Remove pan from oven, and sprinkle with cheese. Return to oven 1-2 minutes or until cheese is melted. Serve immediately.

Yield:

4 servings

Nutrition Information (per serving):

110 calories; 7.5 g fat; 11 mg cholesterol; 356 mg sodium; 6.3 g carbohydrate; 2.0 g fiber; 5.0 g protein

Cook's Comment:

I love this recipe because the blue cheese melts into every crevice of the Brussels sprouts after they've already roasted to a crispy perfection. If you're looking for something other than soggy, bland Brussels sprouts, this recipe will turn you into a Brussels sprouts fanatic! My husband launches himself to the table when these are served up!

Mayo-Free Chicken Salad

1 small (1 lb packed meat) rotisserie chicken,
   skinless
½ cup nonfat plain Greek yogurt
2–3 teaspoons Dijon mustard

Salt and pepper, to taste
2 large celery stalks, finely chopped
3 green onions, chopped
⅓ cup dried cranberries

Directions:

Pick a 1-lb rotisserie chicken, and tear meat into bite-sized pieces. Add yogurt, mustard, salt, and pepper; stir to combine. Fold in remaining ingredients, and refrigerate until served.

Yield:

8 servings (½ cup each)

Nutrition Information (per serving):

134 calories; 8.1 g fat; 37 mg cholesterol; 295 mg sodium;
4.9 g carbohydrate; 0.6 g fiber; 12.3 g protein

Cook's Comment:

It's difficult to believe that a chicken salad with so few ingredients and absolutely no mayonnaise could be so delicious . . . but it is. The Dijon adds flavor, the celery adds crunch, the chicken is moist and flavorful, and the cranberries add the perfect finishing touch.

Pesto Mashed Potatoes in a Portobello Cap

4 portobello mushrooms
1½ lbs medium Yukon Gold potatoes
  (about 5)
¼ cup prepared pesto

¼ cup low-fat buttermilk
¼ cup nonfat plain Greek yogurt
Salt and pepper, to taste

Directions:

Preheat oven to 450°F.

Bring a pot of water to a rolling boil. Meanwhile, peel and dice potatoes; add to boiling water. Boil 20 minutes or until fork-tender.

While potatoes cook, gently wash mushrooms and use a large spoon to scrape gills from the inside of mushroom caps. Place on a baking sheet lined with tinfoil or parchment.

When potatoes are cooked, mash them with a potato masher, or whip them with a hand mixer or in a stand mixer. Add pesto, buttermilk, yogurt, salt, and pepper; combine well.

Spoon mashed potatoes into each of the 4 mushroom caps, and bake 12–15 minutes. Serve immediately.

Yield:

4 pesto mashed potato-stuffed mushrooms

Nutrition Information (per cap):

219 calories; 5.8 g fat; 0 mg cholesterol; 200 mg sodium; 37.8 g carbohydrate; 5.3 g fiber; 9.8 g protein

Fun Fact:

The Bellagio hotel in Las Vegas has a killer buffet that serves pesto mashed potatoes. Judging by the look and taste of them, they're incredibly unhealthy. I lightened up these pesto mashed potatoes and baked them in a portobello mushroom cap. They're cute, healthful, and delicious.

Berry Spinach Salad with Blueberry Vinaigrette

Salad:

12 oz. salad greens or lettuce of choice

½ red onion, thinly sliced

½ cup unsalted walnuts

6 oz. crumbled blue cheese

2 cups strawberries, washed and sliced

1 cup blueberries, washed

1 cup raspberries, washed

Vinaigrette:

¼ cup fresh or froz.en blueberries, thawed

¼ cup red wine vinegar

¼ cup olive oil

½ teaspoon Italian seasoning

1 tablespoon honey

2 cloves garlic

¼ teaspoon salt

Ground black pepper, to taste

Directions:

Blend together vinaigrette ingredients in a blender or food processor; set aside.

In a large bowl, combine salad ingredients. Drizzle with dressing, and toss to coat. Serve immediately.

Yield:

10 servings (1½ cups each)

Nutrition Information (per serving):

185 calories; 13.6 g fat; 13 mg cholesterol; 296 mg sodium; 11.5 g carbohydrate; 2.8 g fiber; 5.3 g protein

Fun Fact:

When I started working in a hospital kitchen and cafeteria, I was amazed at the cook's ability to whip together the most incredible vinaigrettes. The cook used fresh fruits and garlic with olive oil. People go nuts for these salads, which not only include the fabulous vinaigrette, but also rich cheeses, healthful nuts and fresh fruit.

Roasted Winter Squash with Herbed Sugar Glaze

1 (2-lb) butternut squash, peeled and cubed
   (approximately 5 cups)
1 tablespoon olive oil
½ teaspoon salt

¼ teaspoon pepper
¼ cup brown sugar
1 tablespoon rosemary, chopped

Directions:

Preheat oven to 400°F. Line a baking sheet with parchment paper or tinfoil sprayed with olive oil.

Toss cubed squash with olive oil in a medium-sized bowl; toss to coat. Sprinkle with salt and pepper; toss well. Arrange squash on the baking sheet in a single layer.

In a small bowl, combine sugar and rosemary. Using the back of a spoon, grind rosemary into sugar. Sprinkle herbed sugar over squash.

Bake the squash 30–40 minutes or until fork-tender. Serve immediately.

Yield:

5 servings (approximately ⅔ cup each)

Nutrition Information (per serving):

123 calories; 2.8 g fat; 0 mg cholesterol; 235 mg sodium; 25.6 g carbohydrate; 3.0 g fiber; 1.2 g protein

Nutrition Note:

Winter squash is so versatile and packed with flavor that it needs little assistance to be a stellar side, or main, dish on its own. Orange vegetables, like carrots, are packed with vitamin A, and butternut squash is no exception. Butternut squash can be served in sweet or savory dishes, and the squash stays good for a month or two before you cut it.

Paprika Oven Fries

3 large russet or Idaho baking potatoes
2 tablespoons extra-virgin olive oil
2 teaspoons paprika

1 teaspoon garlic salt
Cooking spray

Directions:

Preheat oven to 450°F. Line 2 baking sheets with tinfoil, and spray with cooking spray.

Wash potatoes, and cut into wide fries. Put potatoes into a gallon-sized zip-top bag. Drizzle with olive oil, close, and shake to coat potato pieces on all sides. Sprinkle with paprika and garlic salt, and shake to coat.

Arrange potatoes in a single layer on the baking sheet. Bake 35–40 minutes or until desired crispness is reached. Serve immediately.

Yield:

5 servings (approximately 12–15 fries)

Nutrition Information (per serving):

215 calories; 5.6 g fat; 0 mg cholesterol; 210 mg sodium; 38 g carbohydrate; 4 g fiber; 4.6 g protein

Fun Fact:

Potatoes get a bad reputation, but I have no idea why. Potatoes are loaded with fiber and potassium and are sodium-free. The real issue with potatoes is how we prepare them. Potatoes are the number one most consumed vegetable in the United States and, sadly, the most popular way to prepare potatoes is to make deep-fried french fries full of trans fat. Using a minimal amount of oil and baking your fries is a far more healthful alternative. And they taste great, too!

Watermelon and Arugula Salad

Dressing:

3 tablespoons olive oil

3 tablespoons white balsamic vinegar

¼ teaspoon salt and pepper, to taste

Salad:

8 cups arugula, loosely packed

2 cups watermelon, cubed

¼ red onion, thinly sliced

¼ cup unsalted sunflower seeds, shelled

4 oz. feta cheese crumbled

Cook's Comment:

When you have really bold flavors in a recipe like this, keep the dressing simple to accent the ingredients. For the record, watermelon and feta cheese taste heavenly together!

Directions:

In a small bowl, whisk together olive oil, vinegar, salt, and pepper; set aside.

Combine arugula, watermelon, and onion in a large bowl. Drizzle dressing over salad, and toss well to combine. Top with sunflower seeds and feta. Serve immediately.

Yield:

4 servings (approximately 2 cups each)

Nutrition Information (per serving):

256 calories; 18.5 g fat; 15 mg cholesterol; 489 mg sodium; 14.3 g carbohydrate; 2.5 g fiber; 10 g protein

Creamy Avocado Potato Salad

2 lbs Yukon Gold potatoes, cut into ¾-inch
    chunks
1–2 tablespoons cilantro
1 clove garlic, peeled
1 ripe avocado
1 tablespoon extra-virgin olive oil
Juice of ½ lime

½ teaspoon salt
¼ teaspoon ground cayenne pepper
    (optional)
1 small Roma tomato, seeded and chopped
¼ small red onion, finely diced
¼ English cucumber, finely diced

Directions:

Put potatoes in a pot, and cover with cold water. Cover the pot, and bring the water to a boil. Lower the heat to a rolling boil, and cook 10–15 minutes, until potatoes are easily pierced with a fork but still firm. Drain and rinse with cool water; drain again, and set aside.

Meanwhile, place cilantro and garlic in the food processor, and process for approximately 10 seconds. Add avocado flesh, olive oil, lime juice, salt, and cayenne into the food processor, and puree until smooth, scraping down the sides with a spatula as needed.

Put potatoes, tomato, onion, and cucumbers into a large mixing bowl. Add avocado mixture and combine, but be careful not to mash the potatoes. Taste, and add more salt and lime juice if desired.

Yield:

About 5 cups (approximately 6 servings, ¾ cup each)

Nutrition Information (per cup):

183 calories; 7.2 g fat; 0 mg cholesterol; 196 mg sodium;
31.8 g carbohydrate; 5.5 g fiber; 4.8 g protein

Nutrition Note:

This recipe omits mayonnaise and opts for the even creamier and incredibly healthy alternative of avocado. You can take your ordinary potato salad that is full of saturated fat and turn it into a potato salad that is full of heart-healthy fat . . . and is one stunning shade of green!

Additional Note:

Serve immediately. Avocado is likely to turn brown after contact with oxygen over time.

Broccoli with Light Cheese Sauce

1 head broccoli (approximately 8 cups), washed and cut into florets

3 tablespoons all-purpose flour

1¼ cups nonfat milk

¾ cup 2% cheddar

½ teaspoon salt

Directions:

Bring 2 quarts of water to a boil in a large pot. Add broccoli, and boil 5–6 minutes or until tender but crisp. Transfer to a serving bowl.

Meanwhile, whisk flour and milk together in a saucepan over medium heat. Bring to a simmer, and simmer 5–7 minutes, whisking often to avoid burning on the bottom. Once milk has thickened to a creamy consistency, whisk in cheese and salt; combine until smooth.

Serve cheese sauce over broccoli.

Yield:

6 servings (about 1 heaping cup each)

Nutrition Information (per serving):

111 calories; 3.0 g fat; 11 mg cholesterol; 352 mg sodium; 13.8 g carbohydrate; 2.6 g fiber; 9.5 g protein

Cook's Comment:

Broccoli with no twist can become boring. While cheesy broccoli is perfect for children, adults will enjoy this, too. Using low-fat milk and low-fat cheese makes for a light cheese sauce that turns ordinary broccoli into something people want to eat.

Arugula Salad with Grilled Peaches and Honey Goat Cheese Dressing

Dressing:
¼ cup olive oil
2 tablespoons honey
2 oz. goat cheese, softened
1 tablespoon white balsamic vinegar
⅛ teaspoon salt
Black pepper, to taste

Salad:
5 peaches, washed, halved, and pitted
10 cups spring mix, loosely packed
¼ cup walnuts
2 oz. goat cheese, crumbled

Cook's Comment:

I've wanted to combine goat cheese and honey in a dressing for a really, really long time. It worked beautifully, and this dressing can truly go with any salad ingredients.

Directions:

Whisk together or blend dressing ingredients; set aside.

Preheat grill to medium-high heat. Grill peaches cut-side down until caramelized with char markings, approximately 5 minutes.

Meanwhile, combine spring mix, walnuts, and goat cheese in a large bowl. Top with dressing, and toss to coat. Serve each salad portion with 2 grilled peach halves.

Yield:

5 servings (2 cups salad with 1 peach each)

Nutrition Information (per serving):

291 calories; 19.2 g fat; 12 mg cholesterol; 195 mg sodium; 28.0 g carbohydrate; 5.0 g fiber; 6.6 g protein

In a Bowl

Creamy Roasted Cauliflower and Broccoli Soup

Crock Pot Chicken Tortilla Soup

Spicy Quinoa Mexican Soup

Best Vegetable Soup

Turkey and Black Bean Chili

Lemon Chicken Orzo Soup with Spinach

Roasted Tomato Soup

Slow Cooker Beef Stew

Creamy Roasted Cauliflower and Broccoli Soup

1 large head cauliflower (approximately
    10 cups), cut into florets
2 spears broccoli (approximately 4 cups),
    cut into florets
1 tablespoon olive oil
¾ teaspoon salt, divided
½ teaspoon black pepper, divided
1 head garlic (approximately 6-8 cloves)
1 tablespoon unsalted butter
2 stalks celery, diced

½ yellow onion, diced
1 large carrot, peeled and diced
¼ teaspoon dried thyme leaves
1 tablespoon flour
⅔ cup dry white wine
28 oz. low-sodium vegetable broth
1 bay leaf
1 tablespoon fresh parsley, minced (optional)
½ cup half-and-half

Directions:

Preheat oven to 400°F.

Combine cauliflower and broccoli florets in a 9-by-13-inch baking dish. Toss with olive oil. Sprinkle lightly with ¼ teaspoon salt and ¼ teaspoon pepper.

Cut the top off the head of garlic, and wrap in tinfoil. Place wrapped garlic on the baking sheet. Roast cauliflower, broccoli, and garlic 20–25 minutes.

Meanwhile, heat butter in a cast-iron Dutch oven or medium-large stockpot. Add onion, celery, and carrot. Sauté over medium heat for approximately 10 minutes. Whisk in ½ teaspoon salt, ¼ teaspoon pepper, thyme, and flour, and continue to cook 2 more minutes.

Add wine, mixing to combine with flour mixture. Slowly add in vegetable broth. Add bay leaf. Remove garlic cloves from their skins, and add to the pot whole. Bring mixture to a boil, then reduce heat to medium-low and simmer 10 minutes. Add cauliflower and broccoli, and simmer an additional 5 minutes.

Remove bay leaf. Working in batches, add soup to a blender or food processor, and blend until pureed and smooth, or puree with an immersion blender in the pot.

Stir in half-and-half and parsley. Cook until just heated through. Serve hot.

Yield:

5 servings (1⅓–1½ cups each)

Nutrition Information (per serving):

206 calories; 7.4 g fat; 8 mg cholesterol; 573 mg sodium;
24.4 g carbohydrate; 7.8 g fiber; 7.0 g protein

Cook's Comment:

This soup amazes me more every time I make it. More than any other recipe, the roasting process is what produces such depths of flavor. The finish of half-and-half sends the soup over the top, but it's divine even without. You'll never guess that combining these ingredients into a soup can be so irresistibly good!

Crock Pot Chicken Tortilla Soup

1¼ lbs boneless, skinless chicken breasts

1 (15-oz.) can no-salt-added diced tomatoes

1 (10-oz.) can enchilada sauce

1 medium onion, chopped

1 (4-oz.) can chopped green chilies

1 clove garlic, minced

1½ cups water

1 (15-oz.) can low-sodium chicken broth

1–2 chipotles in adobo, minced

2 teaspoons cumin

1 teaspoon chili powder

¼ teaspoon ground black pepper

1 whole bay leaf

6 whole corn tortillas

Olive oil spray

¼ cup cilantro, chopped

Directions:

In an electric slow cooker, combine chicken and the first 12 ingredients (through bay leaf). Cover, and cook on low 7–9 hours or on high 3–4 hours.

20 minutes before serving, preheat oven to 400°F.

Lightly spray both sides of tortillas with olive oil. Cut tortillas into 2½–by–½-inch strips. Place on a baking sheet. Bake, turning occasionally, until crisp, 5–10 minutes.

Just before serving, stir cilantro into soup. Serve with tortilla strips on top of soup.

Yield:

5 servings (approximately 1½ cups each)

Nutrition Information (per serving):

262 calories; 3.2 g fat; 55 mg cholesterol; 479 mg sodium; 26.4 g carbohydrate; 4.4 g fiber; 29.6 g protein

Shopping Tip:

Canned goods have come a long way with regard to nutrition. Almost any canned good (even condiments!) come in a low-sodium, reduced-sodium, or no-salt-added variety. You don't need to shy away from convenient foods to stay healthy; you just need to know how to choose convenient foods to be healthy!

Spicy Quinoa Mexican Soup

1 poblano pepper

1 red bell pepper

1 jalapeño pepper

1 Anaheim pepper

2 teaspoons olive oil

1 yellow onion, diced

4 cups low-sodium vegetable broth

3 cloves garlic, minced

¾ cup dry quinoa

2 (14.5 oz.) cans low-sodium, fire-roasted, diced tomatoes

1 tablespoon paprika

½ teaspoon chipotle chili powder

½ teaspoon ground coriander

1 teaspoon ground cumin

2 bay leaves

Pinch of ground cinnamon

1–2 chipotle peppers in adobo, finely diced

1 avocado, cut into ½-inch cubes

1 lime, cut into wedges

Directions:

Set your oven to broil at 550°F, or ignite a gas range that has grates to balance peppers.

Place peppers on a baking sheet or over flame, and roast 2–3 minutes or until charred and black. Check frequently to avoid over-burning; rotate to char all sides. Once charred, place peppers in plastic bag, close, and allow to steam approximately 5 minutes. Scrape off charred skin with the blade of a knife, and dice peppers.

Heat a Dutch oven over medium heat, and add olive oil. Once hot, add diced onions, and stir. Keep stirring until onions start to stick, and add 1 tablespoon of vegetable stock. Repeat this step, stirring often for 20–30 minutes, deglazing the pan every so often with a small amount of vegetable stock. Cook onions for 30 minutes or until onions are caramelized.

Meanwhile, combine quinoa and 1½ cups water in a saucepan. Bring to a boil over medium-high heat. Reduce heat, cover, and simmer for approximately 25 minutes or until all liquid is absorbed.

To the Dutch oven, add garlic and heat until fragrant, about 30 seconds. Add remaining vegetable stock, tomatoes, paprika, chili powder, coriander, cumin, bay leaves, cinnamon, chipotle chilies in adobo, and diced peppers. Bring to a boil. Reduce heat, and simmer uncovered 25 minutes, stirring occasionally. Remove bay leaves. Add cooked quinoa, and stir to combine.

Serve with diced avocado and lime wedges.

Yield:

6 servings (approximately 1½ cups each)

Nutrition Information (per serving):

234 calories; 7.8 g fat; 0 mg cholesterol; 508 mg sodium; 36 g carbohydrate; 6.8 g fiber; 6.0 g protein

Nutrition Note:

This soup is vegan, which is appealing for its nutritional content, but often, vegan meals can lack flavor. With the help of charring and the plethora of peppers in this soup, the taste does not fall short. The colors in this soup are stunning, and the addition of quinoa makes it a thick, hearty soup that also is gluten-free. This will stick to your ribs and warm you from the inside out!

Tip:

Omit the jalapeño or chipotles in adobo if you're looking for a mild soup. This one is spicy!

Best Vegetable Soup

1 teaspoon olive oil

1 yellow onion, diced

4 cloves garlic, minced

Dash of dried red pepper flakes

1 teaspoon dried thyme or 2 teaspoons fresh thyme

1 dried bay leaf

¼ teaspoon salt

¼ teaspoon fresh ground black pepper

64 oz. (8 cups) low-sodium chicken stock

1 (28-oz.) can no-salt-added diced tomatoes, with juices

2 large russet potatoes, diced

2 cups carrots (approximately 4), sliced into bite-sized pieces

1 cup celery (about 3 stalks), diced

8 Brussels sprouts, with ends cut off and quartered

1½ cups frozen corn kernels

1 cup frozen green beans

½ cup fresh flat-leaf parsley, minced

1 (10.75-oz.) can condensed tomato soup plus 1 can water

½ lemon, juiced

Directions:

Warm oil over medium heat in a 6-quart Dutch oven or large stockpot. Add onion, and cook until softened (approximately 5 minutes). Add garlic, and cook another minute or so until fragrant. Add red pepper flakes, thyme, salt, pepper, and bay leaf. Continue to cook for another minute or so.

Add in stock and canned tomatoes plus their juices, and stir. Add in potatoes, and stir. Bring to a boil, turn down to simmer, and loosely cover. Simmer until the potatoes are almost tender, approximately 12–15 minutes.

Add in carrots, celery, and Brussels sprouts. Allow to simmer until carrots are almost tender, approximately 10–12 minutes.

Add in frozen corn, green beans, and parsley. Bring back up to simmer, and cook until all vegetables are tender, an additional 10 minutes or so.

Add in condensed soup and water and lemon juice. Season with salt and pepper to taste. Remove bay leaf. Serve immediately.

Yield:

12 servings (2 cups each)

Nutrition Information (per serving):

103 calories; 0.7 g fat; 0 mg cholesterol; 681 mg sodium; 20.9 g carbohydrate; 3 g fiber; 4.3 g protein

Nutrition Note:

This recipe is slightly adapted from Renee Pajestka who blogs over at *My Kitchen Adventures*. It is one good vegetable soup, let me tell you. Of course, there are few things more healthful than vegetable soup. But, sodium can add up quickly. Omitting salt from recipes is a great way to reduce sodium, but choosing a balance among fresh, frozen, and canned also can help. Fresh generally always will be lowest in sodium, with frozen closely behind, and canned products the highest in sodium.

Tip:

To make this a delicious vegan or vegetarian soup, substitute chicken broth for vegetable broth.

Turkey and Black Bean Chili

1 tablespoon olive oil
1 large onion, chopped
1 green bell pepper, seeded and chopped
1 red bell pepper, seeded and chopped
4 garlic cloves, minced
1 lb ground turkey breast
2 (15-oz.) cans black beans, rinsed and
   drained

1 (14½-oz.) can *no-salt-added* diced tomatoes
1 (15-oz.) can tomato sauce
3 tablespoons regular chili powder
1 teaspoon ancho chili powder
1 teaspoon chipotle chili powder
1½ tablespoons ground cumin
1 teaspoon dried oregano

Directions:

Heat the oil in a Dutch oven over medium-high heat. Add onion, bell peppers, and garlic; cook, stirring occasionally, until softened, approximately 5 minutes.

Add turkey and cook, breaking it apart with a wooden spoon until no longer pink, approximately 3 minutes. Stir in beans, tomatoes, tomato sauce, and seasonings; bring to a boil.

Reduce heat and simmer, covered, until vegetables are very tender, about 45 minutes. Serve hot.

Yield:

6 servings (1⅓ cups each)

Nutrition Information (per serving):

298 calories; 5.0 g fat; 33 mg cholesterol; 773 mg sodium; 38.0 g carbohydrate; 13.7 g fiber; 28.0 g protein

Fun Fact:

This chili recipe comes from a long-time reader of my blog, Stacey C. McSweeney. She entered her chili into my blog's annual chili contest, and it took first place. This traditional chili is a winner, and I absolutely love its seasonings. Thanks for sharing your winning recipe, Stacey!

Shopping Tip:

In theory, buying ground turkey should be more healthful than buying ground beef. However, it really depends. Ground beef can be lean, even leaner than ground turkey. Unless you are buying ground turkey breast, the turkey will contain the poultry skin, which is high in calories and saturated fat. By choosing ground turkey breast, your meat will be lean and much lower in calories and fat.

Lemon Chicken Orzo Soup with Spinach

1 teaspoon extra-virgin olive oil

1 medium onion, chopped

4 carrots, halved lengthwise and chopped

3 ribs celery, halved lengthwise and chopped

2 cloves garlic, minced

1 bay leaf

½ teaspoon dried thyme

½ teaspoon dried oregano

3 (32 oz.) cartons (12 cups) low-sodium chicken stock

1 lb rotisserie chicken meat

8 oz. orzo pasta

½ cup fresh lemon juice (about 2 lemons)

Zest from 1 lemon

Black pepper, to taste

8 oz. baby spinach

Directions:

In a large stockpot or Dutch oven, heat oil on medium heat. Add onion, carrots, and celery. Cook until vegetables begin to soften and onion becomes translucent. Add garlic, and cook for 1 minute or so. Add bay leaf, thyme, oregano, and pepper. Cook for another 30 seconds or so, and add broth. Bring to a boil, then partially cover and turn down to a simmer. Cook until vegetables are just soft, approximately 5–6 minutes.

Add pasta, lemon juice, and lemon zest. Stir. Simmer 7–8 minutes.

Add cooked chicken. Allow to heat through. Stir in baby spinach, and allow it to wilt in hot broth. Remove bay leaf, and serve.

Yield:

8 servings (2 cups each)

Nutrition Information (per serving):

246 calories; 2 g fat; 47 mg cholesterol; 214 mg sodium; 31 g carbohydrate; 3.6 g fiber; 24.5 g protein

Fun Fact:

This soup was slightly adapted from a longtime reader of mine, Renee Pajestka. Her vegetable soup recipe is also part of this section. In short, her soups are incredible, and I changed this recipe very little to suit my preferences. You'll be blown away at how flavorful this soup is . . . and the lemon twist can brighten a winter day.

Roasted Tomato Soup

3 lbs Roma tomatoes (about 12), halved
   lengthwise
½ teaspoon salt
½ teaspoon pepper
2 tablespoons extra-virgin olive oil
4 garlic cloves, unpeeled

1 teaspoon fresh thyme, finely chopped
   (or ¼ teaspoon dried)
2 teaspoons fresh oregano, finely chopped
   (or ½ teaspoon dried)
4 cups low-sodium vegetable stock
1 cup 2% milk

Directions:

Preheat oven to 400°F.

Place tomatoes, cut-side facing up, on a baking sheet. Sprinkle with salt and pepper. Drizzle tomatoes with olive oil. Toss in garlic cloves, and roast 1 hour.

Peel garlic, and transfer cloves, tomatoes, and any accumulated juices to a blender, food processor, or stockpot with an immersion blender, and puree until desired consistency is achieved.

Transfer puree to a stockpot with herbs and broth; bring to a boil. Reduce heat to a simmer, and cook, uncovered, 25 minutes. Remove from heat, and stir in milk.

Yield:

5 servings (approximately 1½ cups each)

Nutrition Information (per serving):

143 calories; 7.0 g fat; 4.0 mg cholesterol; 367 mg sodium; 17.0 g carbohydrate; 4.2 g fiber; 5.0 g protein

Cook's Comment:

I love Roma or plum tomatoes, because they are meaty and are not chock-full of seeds and slimy insides like many larger tomato varieties. Consistently, they seem to be the best-tasting tomato variety, as well as one of the most affordable.

Slow Cooker Beef Stew

1¼ lbs stewing beef, trimmed and cut into 1-inch cubes

1 tablespoon olive oil

1 (15-oz.) can no-salt–added diced tomatoes

1 yellow onion, chopped into large pieces

1 rib celery, chopped

2 carrots, peeled and chopped

10 small potatoes (approximately 1½ lbs), halved

1 teaspoon Italian seasoning

2 cups low-sodium beef broth

2 bay leaves

1 cup frozen peas

½ teaspoon salt

¼ teaspoon black pepper

Directions:

Heat olive oil in a large skillet over medium-high heat. Once hot, add beef to the skillet and brown, approximately 5 minutes. Remove from heat, and set aside.

Add tomatoes, onion, celery, carrots, and potatoes to slow cooker. Sprinkle Italian seasoning over vegetables, then add beef and any accumulated juices. Pour beef broth over top of beef and vegetables. Add bay leaves.

Cover slow cooker with lid, and cook on low 8–10 hours.

About 20 minutes before serving, add peas, salt, and pepper. Remove bay leaves before serving.

Yield:

6 servings (about 1½ heaping cups each)

Nutrition Information (per serving):

290 calories; 7.3 g fat; 50 mg cholesterol; 461 mg sodium; 31.7 g carbohydrate 5.0 g fiber; 22.5 g protein

Cook's Comment:

I didn't care for stew . . . until I tried this recipe. Stewing meat is incredibly lean (and affordable), making it perfectly suited for slow cookers. This stew can cook all day and only gets better and better. Other than meat, this meal is full of vegetables, and thus, fiber. Meals with fewer than 300 calories are hard to come by, but meals with fewer than 300 calories that top the favorites charts are nearly unheard of!

From Land and Sea

Pizza Burgers

Baked Chicken Parmesan

California Roll Lettuce Roll-Ups

Creamy Pesto Chicken Enchiladas

Baked Honey Dijon Salmon

Shrimp Pad Thai

Cod Picatta

Grilled Pork Tenderloin in a Honey-Soy Marinade

Quick Tex-Mex Chicken Packets

Shrimp in Lemon Horseradish Sauce

Grilled Chicken with Bruschetta Topping

Salmon with Pomegranate Reduction

Herb-Baked Chicken with Roasted Tomatoes

Parmesan Tilapia

Slow Cooker Honey Sesame Chicken with Green Beans and Rice

Lemonade Salmon with Creamy Russian Dressing

Zucchini-Sausage Pizza

Spicy Citrus-Soy Flank Steak

Chicken and Couscous in Tomato-Basil Broth

Chipotle Shrimp and Poblano Tostadas

Slow-cooked Pork Carnitas Tacos

Halibut with Cold Cucumber Salad

Coconut Shrimp and Chickpea Curry

Pizza Burgers

Burgers:

1½ lbs 96% lean ground beef

1 tablespoon olive oil

¼ small onion, grated

1 clove garlic, minced

1 tablespoon balsamic vinegar

2 teaspoons dried Italian seasoning

6 oz. fresh mozzarella cheese, thinly sliced

6 whole-wheat hamburger buns, split and
toasted or grilled

Pizza Sauce:

1 teaspoon extra-virgin olive oil

2 cloves garlic, minced

1 (14.5-oz.) can no-salt-added diced
tomatoes, undrained

2 tablespoons tomato paste

½ teaspoon dried Italian seasoning

½ teaspoon sugar

¼ teaspoon salt

Pinch black pepper

Directions:

For pizza sauce, heat oil in a medium-sized saucepan over medium heat. Once hot, add garlic, and cook until fragrant, about 30–60 seconds. Add the rest of sauce ingredients, and cook until thickened, approximately 5 minutes, stirring frequently. Keep warm.

To make burgers, combine ground beef, oil, onion, garlic, vinegar, and Italian seasoning in a large bowl. Divide meat into 6 portions, and shape each into a patty.

Grill burgers over medium-high heat until done, about 4–5 minutes per side. When burgers have about 2 minutes left to cook, spoon approximately 3 tablespoons pizza sauce on top of each, and then top each with 1 oz. mozzarella. Cover grill so cheese melts.

Transfer burgers onto buns, and serve immediately.

Yield:

6 burgers

Nutrition Information (per serving):

416 calories; 15.0 g fat; 75 mg cholesterol; 571 mg sodium; 37.0 g carbohydrate; 8.7 g fiber; 37.8 g protein

Nutrition Note:

Burgers actually can be healthy. . . . Yep, you read that right. Buying extra-lean ground beef ensures you're watching calories and fat. However, extra-lean meat can become dry easily. To keep burgers moist—and healthful—try adding healthy oils, such as olive oil, to your burger patties. You'll love it!

Tip:

Use gluten-free buns to make this recipe appropriate for gluten-free eaters!

Baked Chicken Parmesan

1 teaspoon olive oil

⅔ cup panko bread crumbs

¼ cup ground flaxseed

1 tablespoon grated Parmesan cheese

⅓ cup all-purpose flour

1 teaspoon garlic powder

½ teaspoon salt and pepper

2 large egg whites

1 tablespoon water

Nonstick cooking spray

1 large (8-oz.) boneless, skinless chicken
   breast, halved widthwise to create
   thinner breasts

½ cup marinara

¼ cup part-skim mozzarella cheese,
   shredded

Directions:

Preheat oven to 475°F. Fit a wire cooling rack over a baking sheet, and spray with oil; set aside.

Heat a small skillet over medium heat, and add oil. When oil is hot, stir in panko, and stir often, until golden brown, approximately 5–6 minutes. Transfer panko to a shallow dish, and cool slightly; when cool, stir in flaxseed and grated Parmesan.

In a second shallow dish, combine flour, garlic powder, ½ teaspoon salt, and ½ teaspoon pepper. In a third shallow dish, whisk together egg whites and water.

Lightly dredge cutlets in flour, shaking off any excess flour. Next, dip chicken cutlets into egg whites, and finally coat with panko and flaxseed. Arrange chicken on the wire cooling rack, and bake 15 minutes.

Remove chicken from oven. Ladle ¼ cup marinara and 2 tablespoons cheese onto each cutlet. Return them to oven, and continue to bake until cheese has melted, approximately 2–3 minutes.

Yield:

2 servings (5 oz. each)

Nutrition Information (per serving):

395 calories; 11.5 g fat; 72 mg cholesterol; 698 mg sodium; 30.0 g carbohydrate; 3.5 g fiber; 44.0 g protein

Nutrition Note:

I love being sneaky. All the nutritional perks of ground flaxseed, like omega-3 fatty acids, bind well to the egg whites to boost the nutritional value of this classic hit recipe. The panko adds a crunch, and keeping the marinara and cheese portioned helps reduce calories and sodium.

California Roll Lettuce Roll-Ups

1 cup dry white rice

2 tablespoons seasoned rice vinegar

1 head Boston lettuce (approximately 12 leaves), with leaves removed and washed

½ English cucumber, seeded and chopped into 1-inch sticks

½ cup carrot (approximately 2), shredded

5 oz. surimi (imitation crab meat), chopped into 1-inch sticks

½ avocado, diced

3 tablespoons picked ginger, chopped

2 tablespoons low-sodium soy sauce

Directions:

In a small saucepan, bring 2 cups water and a pinch of salt to a boil. Stir in rice, cover, and reduce heat. Simmer rice 20–40 minutes, according to package directions. Once cooked, stir in vinegar, and set aside.

To assemble roll-ups, layer several tablespoons rice in each lettuce leaf. Layer on 2–3 pieces of cucumber, carrot, crab, and avocado. Top with pickled ginger and a dash of low-sodium soy sauce.

Yield:

4 servings (3 roll-ups each)

Nutrition Information (per serving):

255 calories; 3.5 g fat; 2 mg cholesterol; 704 mg sodium; 50 g carbohydrate; 2.5 g fiber; 7.5 g protein

Fun Fact:

Sushi is one food I love, but also one that I am unlikely to attempt at home. These California rolls were made into lettuce roll-ups that are colorful, light, and healthful. Another fun idea is to make sushi bowls by throwing all the ingredients of sushi into bowls of rice and voila!

Creamy Pesto Chicken Enchiladas

¼ cup pesto

6 oz. low-fat cream cheese

1 cup low-fat ricotta

½ teaspoon salt

3 Roma tomatoes, seeded and diced

1 lb boneless, skinless chicken breasts, cooked and shredded

8 oz. fresh mozzarella, diced and divided

12 6-inch whole–wheat flour tortillas

Directions:

Preheat oven to 350°F.

In a large bowl or the bowl of a stand mixer, combine pesto, cream cheese, ricotta, and salt. Mix with a hand mixer, or mix on medium speed with a whisk attachment until combined, scraping down sides as needed. Set aside ½ cup of mixture. Fold in tomatoes, chicken, and 4 oz. mozzarella.

Spoon approximately ¼ cup chicken-pesto mixture into each tortilla, and roll. Place enchiladas seam-side down into the prepared baking dish. Repeat with remaining tortillas and filling.

Spread reserved pesto mixture over enchiladas using a rubber spatula, and sprinkle with remaining 4 oz. mozzarella.

Cover baking dish with tinfoil, and bake 20–25 minutes. Allow to cool 5 minutes before serving.

Yield:

6 servings (2 enchiladas each)

Nutrition Information (per serving):

472 calories; 17.5 g fat; 83 mg cholesterol; 644 mg sodium; 38.2 g carbohydrate; 4.7 g fiber; 37.3 g protein

Fun Fact:

Mozzarella cheese is naturally low in calories and fat (including saturated fat); plus, it melts beautifully. I am a proponent for creating a pesto version of nearly every dish, and with enchiladas being one of my favorite . . . well, it was just meant to be! I tried these with corn and flour tortillas, and I must say, the corn-plus-pesto flavor wasn't appealing. This is one instance when flour tortillas are the way to go.

Baked Honey Dijon Salmon

2 tablespoons unsalted butter, melted
3 tablespoons Dijon mustard
2 tablespoons honey
¼ cup panko bread crumbs

2 tablespoons walnuts, chopped
2 tablespoons fresh parsley, minced
4 (5 oz.) wild Alaskan salmon filets
1 lemon, for garnish

Directions:

Preheat oven to 400°F.

In a small bowl, stir together butter, mustard, and honey. Set aside. In another bowl, mix bread crumbs, walnuts, and parsley.

Brush each salmon filet lightly with honey mustard mixture, and sprinkle tops of filets with bread-crumb mixture.

Bake salmon 12–15 minutes in preheated oven or until it flakes easily with a fork. Garnish with a wedge of lemon, and serve immediately.

Yield:

4 servings

Nutrition Information (per serving):

407 calories; 24.3 g fat; 88 mg cholesterol; 340 mg sodium;
15 g carbohydrate; 0.8 g fiber; 31.3 g protein

Cook's Comment:

While I love salmon just as it is, it's fun to dress up your favorites sometimes. I deem this recipe the perfect choice for trying to covert someone into a salmon-lover. The bold flavors and varying textures are very pleasing and the smell of this baking . . . mmmm!

 This is another recipe that easily can be made into a gluten-free meal simply by using gluten-free bread!

Shrimp Pad Thai

3 tablespoons solid tamarind
¾ cup boiling water
3 tablespoons fish sauce
1 tablespoon seasoned rice vinegar
3 tablespoons granulated sugar
¾ teaspoon cayenne pepper
4 tablespoons peanut oil
8 oz. dried rice stick noodles
2 large eggs

1 lb large shrimp, peeled and deveined
3 cloves garlic, minced
1 medium shallot, minced
6 tablespoons unsalted peanuts
3 cups (6 oz.) bean sprouts
5 scallions, sliced thin
¼ cup fresh cilantro leaves, chopped
1 lime, cut into wedges

Directions:

Soak tamarind in ¾ cup boiling water for approximately 10 minutes. Push tamarind through a mesh strainer; discard any stringy solids. Stir fish sauce, rice vinegar, sugar, cayenne, and 2 tablespoons peanut oil into tamarind liquid, and set aside.

Meanwhile, cover rice sticks with hot tap water in a large bowl; soak until softened, pliable, and limp but not fully tender, approximately 20 minutes. Drain noodles, and set aside.

Beat eggs in a small bowl; set aside.

Heat 1 tablespoon oil in a large skillet over high heat until just beginning to smoke, approximately 2 minutes. Add shrimp and cook, tossing occasionally, until shrimp are opaque and browned about the edges, about 3 minutes. Transfer shrimp to a plate, and set aside.

To the same skillet, add remaining 1 tablespoon oil to skillet, and swirl to coat; add garlic and shallot, set skillet over medium heat, and cook, stirring constantly, until light golden brown, approximately 1½ minutes. Add eggs to skillet, and stir with wooden spoon until lightly scrambled, about 20 seconds. Add noodles to eggs; toss to combine. Pour fish sauce mixture over noodles, increase heat to high, and cook, tossing constantly, until noodles are evenly coated. Scatter ¼ cup peanuts, bean sprouts, all but ¼ cup scallions, and cooked shrimp over noodles; continue to cook, tossing constantly, until noodles are tender, approximately 3 minutes.

Transfer noodles to a serving platter; sprinkle with remaining scallions, 2 tablespoons peanuts, and cilantro; serve hot with a lime wedge.

Yield:

5 servings (about 1⅓ cups each)

Nutrition Information (per serving):

498 calories; 19 g fat; 206 mg cholesterol; 963 mg sodium; 58.6 g carbohydrate; 4.2 g fiber; 28 g protein

Fun Fact:

I have tried about twenty Pad Thai recipes, but this one is best. The YMCA on campus at the University of Illinois at Urbana-Champaign always sold authentic Thai food. I would get Tofu Pad Thai every Friday. I'm obsessed with the stuff. The unique blend of flavors is out of this world—and don't even try to replicate the flavors of tamarind with another ingredient . . . it won't work. Check out local ethnic markets for tamarind that comes in blocks of thick, heavy, dark, meaty pulp. Or try online retailers! This ingredient makes or breaks a Thai dish and is worth the search.

Cod Piccata

2 (5-oz.) cod filets

⅛ teaspoon salt

Pinch of pepper

3 tablespoons all-purpose flour

1 tablespoon unsalted butter

1 tablespoon olive oil

Juice of ½ lemon

¼ cup dry white wine

¼ cup low-sodium chicken broth

2 tablespoons capers, drained and rinsed

Directions:

Season cod with salt and pepper on both sides. Spoon flour into a shallow bowl, and dredge fish on both sides, patting flour to stick. Reserve any excess flour.

In a medium skillet, heat butter and oil over medium-high heat. Once hot, add the fish and sear 3–4 minutes per side; transfer fish onto a plate, and cover with tinfoil to keep warm.

To the skillet, add lemon juice, wine, broth, and capers. Over medium heat, whisk piccata sauce until boiling. Add 2 teaspoons of the reserved flour, and whisk until smooth and thickened, about 3–4 minutes. Return cod to sauce; serve hot with piccata drizzled over fish.

Yield:

2 servings

Nutrition Information (per serving):

332 calories; 14 g fat; 84 mg cholesterol; 394 mg; 11.0 g carbohydrate; 0 g fat; 25 g protein

Nutrition Note:

Piccata is a classic sauce that packs tons of flavor with its bold ingredients—lemon juice, butter, and capers. Choosing a lean but "meaty" fish like cod makes it perfect for balancing out the meal in terms of fat and calories. Cutting back on butter and oil and substituting wine and broth does no injustice to piccata. I even prefer it!

Grilled Pork Tenderloin in a Honey-Soy Marinade

1 lb tenderloin, trimmed of fat

2 cloves garlic, minced

2 tablespoons honey

2 tablespoons low-sodium soy sauce

⅛ teaspoon ground mustard

Cook's Comment:

Sometimes marinades get too complicated. The beauty of marinades is the hands-off approach anyway, right? Right. This recipe keeps it simple . . . and full of flavor. Remember, pork tenderloin also can be made in a cooking bag and baked, or seared over the stove top in a bit of oil and baked off to finish.

Directions:

Combine garlic, honey, soy sauce, and ground mustard in a small bowl, whisking well. Transfer marinade to a zip-top bag, and add tenderloin. Marinade in the refrigerator for at least 2 hours but no longer than 24 hours.

Preheat grill to medium heat.

Grill tenderloin on each of 4 sides, about 5 minutes per side. Transfer tenderloin onto a cutting board, and cover with tinfoil. Allow to sit 5–10 minutes before slicing.

Yield:

4 servings (3½ oz. each)

Nutrition Information (per serving):

140 calories; 3.5 g fat; 65 mg cholesterol; 284 mg sodium; 5.8 g carbohydrate; 0 g fiber; 21.3 g protein

Quick Tex-Mex Chicken Packets

¾ lb boneless, skinless chicken breasts, cubed

Juice of ½ lime

1 teaspoon cumin

½ teaspoon chili powder

Pinch of cayenne

1 (15-oz.) can black beans, drained and rinsed

1 cup frozen corn

½ green bell pepper, diced

½ red bell pepper, diced

⅔ cup salsa

½ cup cilantro, chopped

Directions:

Preheat oven to 400°F. Rip off 3 sheets of parchment or tinfoil, each 2 feet long; set aside.

In a medium-sized bowl, combine cubed chicken and lime juice; toss to coat. Add in spice, tossing well. Stir in remaining ingredients.

Divide mixture into the middle of each of the 3 pieces of parchment or tinfoil, bringing the 2 sides together, folding down, and tucking the ends under the weight of the packet. Arrange packets on a baking sheet, and bake 30–35 minutes.

Cut packets, or transfer contents onto a plate. Serve hot.

Yield:

3 servings

Nutrition Information (per serving):

331 calories; 3.0 g fat; 55 mg cholesterol; 565 mg sodium;
40 g carbohydrate; 9.7 g fiber; 36.7 g protein

Cook's Comment:

Not only are these kid-friendly, but they also can be prepared 1–2 days ahead of time for a dinner that's ready in a flash!

Shrimp in Lemon Horseradish Sauce

½ lemon, thinly sliced

¼ teaspoon salt

1 teaspoon whole peppercorns

4 sprigs dill

1 lb large raw shrimp, thawed if frozen

1 tablespoon lemon juice, freshly squeezed

1 tablespoon Dijon mustard

2 teaspoons olive oil

2 teaspoons prepared horseradish

2 tablespoons plain nonfat Greek yogurt

2 teaspoons fresh dill, minced

3 green onions, thinly sliced

Directions:

Fill a wide, deep sauté pan with 1–2 inches of water. Add lemon slices, salt, peppercorns, and dill; bring to a boil.

Meanwhile, mix lemon juice, mustard, olive oil, horseradish, yogurt, and dill in a small bowl.

Reduce heat to a simmer, and poach shrimp in boiling water for approximately 3–4 minutes or until cooked through. Drain shrimp, and add to bowl with yogurt mixture; toss to coat. Serve immediately.

Yield:

4 servings (4 oz. each)

Nutrition Information (per serving):

153 calories; 4.3 g fat; 150 mg cholesterol; 404 mg sodium; 2.8 g carbohydrate; 0.5 g fiber; 23.8 g protein

Cook's Comment:

Poaching is a fat-free method of cooking that is not used often enough by the home cook. Boiling water with herbs and spices can make for a quick and healthful means of preparing foods, especially seafood and vegetables.

Grilled Chicken with Bruschetta Topping

¼ cup red onion, chopped

1 tablespoon extra-virgin olive oil

1 tablespoon balsamic vinegar

¼ teaspoon salt and pepper, to taste

2 large vine-ripe tomatoes, chopped

2 cloves garlic, minced

2 tablespoons fresh basil leaves, chopped

4 oz. fresh mozzarella, diced

4 (4 oz.) boneless, skinless chicken breasts

Directions:

In a medium-sized bowl, combine onion, olive oil, balsamic vinegar, salt, and pepper. Add tomatoes, garlic, basil, and cheese to onion mixture. Set aside.

Season chicken with a pinch of salt and pepper, and grill on your indoor or outdoor grill. Top chicken with bruschetta, and serve immediately.

Yield:

4 servings

Nutrition Information (per serving):

259 calories; 10.8 g fat; 75 mg cholesterol; 242 mg sodium; 6.5 g carbohydrate; 1.3 g fiber; 32 g protein

Nutrition Note:

Everyone makes bruschetta a little differently, but in my opinion, balsamic vinegar is the key ingredient. Along with great tomatoes, of course. Using vinegar in bruschetta helps add a ton of flavor with very few calories. You can make bruschetta for an appetizer and, the following day, turn it into dinner. What's easier than that?

Salmon with Pomegranate Reduction

Olive oil cooking spray
2 (5 oz.) salmon filets
⅛ teaspoon salt

⅛ teaspoon pepper
½ cup 100% pomegranate juice
2 tablespoons pomegranate arils

Directions:

Preheat oven to 400°F. Line a baking sheet with tinfoil or parchment, and mist with olive-oil cooking spray.

Arrange salmon, skin-side down, onto the baking sheet. Sprinkle with salt and pepper. Bake salmon 12–14 minutes or until a muted, dull pink.

Meanwhile, heat pomegranate juice over medium heat. Bring to a boil, and reduce heat to low, whisking often to avoid burning. The juice will thicken and become reduced by half. Stir in pomegranate arils.

Remove salmon from oven and plate. Drizzle pomegranate reduction and arils over top of each salmon filet. Serve immediately.

Yield:

2 servings

Nutrition Information (per serving):

290 calories; 12 g fat; 90 mg cholesterol; 215 mg sodium; 0.5 g fiber; 30 g protein

Shopping Tip:

Fresh pomegranate juice commonly is found in the refrigerated produce section in grocery stores. It is full of flavor and perfect for fall-inspired meals. Pomegranate arils are juicy, tart seeds that make up the pomegranate fruit itself. They are in season in the fall and add a fun crunch and tart flavor to salads, sauces, and beyond!

Herb-Baked Chicken with Roasted Tomatoes

4 lbs roasting chicken
10–20 sprigs thyme
5 cloves garlic, peeled
½ bulb fennel, sliced
1 handful fresh parsley

20 basil leaves
1 tablespoon olive oil
½ teaspoon salt
¼ teaspoon pepper
1 pint cherry tomatoes

Directions:

Preheat oven to 425°F.

Remove giblets from chicken. Rinse chicken under cold running water. Pat dry.

Arrange thyme in the bottom of a roasting pan; set chicken on top. Stuff chicken with garlic, fennel, parsley, and basil. Drizzle olive oil over chicken, and cover surface of chicken with oil using a brush. Sprinkle with salt and pepper.

Arrange tomatoes around the roasting pan surrounding chicken.

Bake 1½ hours. Remove roasting pan and chicken from oven and carefully cover with tinfoil. Allow to rest 20 minutes before serving.

Yield:

6 servings (about 4 oz. meat and 4–5 tomatoes)

Nutrition Information (per serving):

214 calories; 14.2 g fat; 70 mg cholesterol; 246 mg sodium; 3.0 g carbohydrate; 0.8 g fiber; 18.7 g protein

Cook's Comment:

Roasting a chicken is simple—don't let it scare you! Stuff the chicken with whichever seasonings or vegetables you have around, and pop it in the oven. The tomatoes in this dish turn out beautifully as they slow-cook and soak in the flavors of thyme.

Parmesan Tilapia

4 (4 oz.) tilapia filets
¼ cup (1 oz.) Parmesan cheese, shredded
2 tablespoons unsalted butter, softened
1 tablespoon nonfat plain Greek yogurt
1 tablespoon lemon juice

1 clove garlic, minced
¼ teaspoon dried Italian seasoning
¼ teaspoon salt and ground black pepper,
    to taste

Directions:

Pre-heat the oven broiler (500–550°F). Line a baking pan with tinfoil, and spray with cooking spray.

In a small bowl, combine all ingredients except fish. Mix well, and set aside.

Arrange tilapia filets in a single layer on a baking pan. Broil a few inches from heat for 2–3 minutes. Flip filets over, and broil for an additional 2–3 minutes.

Remove from oven, and cover top side of filets with Parmesan cheese mixture. Return to broiler, and continue cooking, 1–2 minutes, until top is lightly browned.

Yield:

4 tilapia filets

Nutrition Information (per filet):

182 calories; 8.5 g fat; 6 mg cholesterol; 313 mg sodium;
0.8 g carbohydrate; 0.1 g fiber; 25.5 g protein

Cook's Comment:

Mild-flavored fish like tilapia offer a blank slate for taking on flavors. Because of the thin cut of most tilapia, it cooks quickly and makes for a meal that's ready in minutes. Between the butter and cheese, this fish is ideal for those still developing a palate for seafood. It's sure to win them over!

Slow Cooker Honey Sesame Chicken with Green Beans and Rice

4 boneless, skinless chicken breasts (1¼ lbs)
⅓ cup honey
2 tablespoons low-sodium soy sauce
½ onion, diced
2 tablespoons ketchup
2 teaspoons toasted sesame oil
3 cloves garlic, minced, pressed, or grated

½ teaspoon red pepper flakes
2 tablespoons cornstarch
1 cup dry basmati rice
1 teaspoon extra-virgin olive oil
1 lb green beans, trimmed and halved
1 tablespoon sesame seeds

Directions:

Put chicken into slow cooker.

In a small bowl, combine honey, soy sauce, onion, ketchup, oil, garlic, and pepper flakes; whisk to combine. Pour over chicken.

Cook on low 3–4 hours or on high 1½–2½ hours, just until chicken is cooked through.

Cook rice according to package directions.

Trim green beans. Heat 1 teaspoon olive oil in a skillet until hot. Add green beans, and sauté 5–6 minutes or until cooked and al dente.

Remove chicken from slow cooker; leave sauce. Whisk cornstarch into liquid in slow cooker. Replace lid, and cook sauce on high 5–10 minutes or until slightly thickened.

Shred chicken or cut into bite-sized pieces, then return to pot and toss with sauce. Serve chicken over rice with green beans; garnish with sesame seeds.

Yield:

4 servings (¾ cup rice with 5 oz. chicken/sauce and ⅔ cup green beans)

Nutrition Information (per serving):

482 calories; 5.8 g fat; 69 mg cholesterol; 435 mg sodium; 70.3 g carbohydrate; 2.5 g fiber; 37.3 g protein

Cook's Comment:

I refer to honey, soy sauce, and toasted sesame oil as "the trifecta of Asian flavors." When you combine the three, there's really no going wrong. This recipe is a favorite, and it's easy to make. I even like to throw the green beans into the slow cooker with the chicken and sauce to distribute the finger-licking-good flavors to the vegetables, too!

Lemonade Salmon with Creamy Russian Dressing

Salmon:

1 lb salmon filet, with skin on

8 oz. (1 cup) 100% fruit juice lemonade

½ teaspoon salt and pepper to taste

Russian Dressing:

2 tablespoons light mayonnaise

2 tablespoons nonfat plain Greek yogurt

1 tablespoon ketchup

1 tablespoon red wine vinegar

1 teaspoon prepared horseradish

2 teaspoons Worcestershire sauce

½ teaspoon onion powder

Directions:

Preheat oven to 500°F. Line a 9-by-13-inch pan with parchment paper or tinfoil. Sprinkle salmon with salt and pepper. Pour lemonade into pan. Place salmon in juice. Loosely place parchment paper or tinfoil over salmon. Roast 15 minutes.

While salmon is cooking, prepare Russian dressing. In a medium-sized bowl, combine mayonnaise, ketchup, horseradish, Worcestershire sauce, dill relish, and onion salt. Mix well, and refrigerate until ready to serve.

Yield:

4 servings (4 oz. each)

Nutrition Information (per serving):

236 calories; 11.3 g fat; 75 mg cholesterol; 350 mg sodium; 6.3 g carbohydrate; 0 g fiber; 24.8 g protein

Cook's Comment:

When a recipe calls for mayonnaise, I like to substitute plain Greek yogurt—sometimes for all the mayonnaise, sometimes for half, sometimes for just a bit. While this is to help cut calories, fat, and sodium, it also creates a unique tanginess that is hard to replicate with any other ingredient. You'll love it!

Zucchini-Sausage Pizza

Dough:

1 tablespoon yeast

1 cup lukewarm water

Pinch of sugar

1½ cups whole-wheat pastry flour or white wheat flour

1½ cups all-purpose flour

1 teaspoon coarse sea salt

2 tablespoons olive oil

Pizza:

2 spicy Italian turkey sausage links, with casings removed

1 medium zucchini, sliced thinly

1 cup pizza sauce

1½ cups 2% mozzarella cheese, shredded

¼ cup Parmesan cheese

Freshly ground pepper

Directions:

In a small bowl, mix yeast with ¼ cup lukewarm water. Add pinch of sugar.

In a large bowl, mix flours and sea salt. Add olive oil, ¾ cup lukewarm water, and yeast mixture. Stir with a wooden spoon until dough gets too stiff, then incorporate the rest of the flour with your hands. Knead 5–10 minutes. Cover with a damp cloth, and let rise 1–2 hours.

Flour dough, form it into a ball, and let rise on a floured surface, covered with a damp cloth, for 20 minutes.

Pre-heat oven to 350°F.

In the meantime, heat a small, nonstick skillet, and sauté sausage, breaking it into crumbles with a spatula until it's cooked through. Transfer sausage onto a paper towel, and sauté zucchini 5–6 minutes to soften and release moisture.

Stretch out on a pizza peel, parchment paper, or baking sheet to 16 inches in diameter. Par-bake crust 4–6 minutes.

Increase oven temperature to 450°F.

Spread sauce over pizza surface, and sprinkle with mozzarella. Layer the par-baked crust with zucchini slices. Sprinkle sausage on top, along with Parmesan cheese, and freshly ground pepper. Bake 10 minutes or until nicely browned. Cool 5 minutes before slicing.

Yield:

8 slices

Nutrition Information (per slice):

312 calories; 10.8 g fat; 30 mg cholesterol; 788 mg sodium; 36.9 g carbohydrate; 3.0 g fiber; 14.3 g protein

Nutrition Note:

Pizza dough is one carbohydrate that is difficult to replicate in a whole-wheat variety. All the 100 percent whole-wheat dough I've ever made is so dense and dry that I've opted for a half whole-wheat variation that yields great results. Sneaking in half whole-wheat flour is something your family won't even notice while you're boosting the fiber and nutrient content of pizza substantially.

Spicy Citrus-Soy Flank Steak

1 lb flank steak, trimmed

Juice of 2 limes

1 tablespoon honey

2 teaspoons toasted sesame oil

1 tablespoon low-sodium soy sauce

1 teaspoon crushed red pepper

Directions:

In a large zip-top bag, combine lime juice, honey, sesame oil, soy sauce, and crushed red pepper. Add flank steak to the bag, and marinade 3–4 hours.

Preheat grill to medium-high heat. When hot, add meat. Grill 5–6 minutes per side for medium-well; allow meat to rest 2–3 minutes. Slice steak against the grain into pieces, and serve hot.

Yield:

4 servings (about 3½ oz. cooked)

Nutrition Information (per serving):

224 calories; 11.3 g fat; 60 mg cholesterol; 215 mg sodium; 6.5 g carbohydrate; 0 g fiber; 23.3 g protein

Cook's Comment:

Flank steak is lean, which can make it tough. By marinating in an acid (lime juice), this steak takes on all the flavors of the marinade while being tender enough to cut with a fork. The Asian flavors and bit of spice make for a marinade that is perfect for any protein, so get creative!

Chicken and Couscous in Tomato-Basil Broth

1 cup dry couscous

4 (4 oz.) boneless, skinless chicken breasts, pounded to ½-inch thickness

¼ teaspoon salt, pepper, dry Italian seasoning, to taste

1 tablespoon olive oil

4 cloves garlic, minced

1 onion, chopped

4 large tomatoes, chopped

2 tablespoons balsamic vinegar

1½ cups low-sodium chicken broth

Handful of fresh basil, cut into chiffonade

6 oz. fresh mozzarella, cubed small

Cook's Comment:

Couscous isn't my favorite grain, but in this dish, it's heavenly! The broth takes on all the flavors of the chicken, tomatoes, garlic, and onion, and the couscous absorbs it all, making the texture smooth and creamy. This is one seriously impressive dish and is perfect to wow your loved ones!

Directions:

Cook couscous according to package directions.

Season chicken with salt, pepper, and Italian seasoning. Heat olive oil in a large skillet over medium-high heat. Add chicken, and brown 4 minutes per side. Transfer to a plate, and cover with tinfoil to keep warm.

Add garlic and onions to pan; sauté 2 minutes. Add tomatoes, and sauté another 2 minutes. Add balsamic vinegar; mix, and allow to cook until fragrant, approximately 30 seconds. Add chicken broth and half the basil. Bring to a steady simmer. Return chicken to pan, and let simmer 5 minutes.

Serve chicken over couscous; top with tomato broth, basil, and fresh mozzarella.

Yield:

4 servings (approximately ¾ cup couscous, 1 chicken breast, and 1½ oz. mozzarella)

Nutrition Information (per serving):

479 calories; 12.3 g fat; 78 mg cholesterol; 251 mg sodium; 47.8 g carbohydrate; 4.8 g fiber; 44 g protein

Chipotle Shrimp and Poblano Tostadas

2 teaspoons olive oil

1 lb shrimp, peeled, deveined, and roughly chopped into ½-inch bites

1 poblano pepper, diced

1 teaspoon cumin

½ teaspoon chipotle chili powder

Pinch of cayenne

6 (6-inch) tostadas

4 cups lettuce, shredded

½ cup tomatoes, diced

1 avocado, diced

½ cup salsa

6 tablespoons nonfat plain Greek yogurt

6 tablespoons (1.5 oz.) Cojita cheese, shredded

Directions:

In a medium skillet, heat olive oil over medium heat. When hot, add shrimp, poblano pepper, and spices. Cook shrimp, stirring occasionally, until pink and no longer opaque, approximately 4–5 minutes.

Layer about 2½ oz. of shrimp and peppers onto each of 6 tostadas. Top each with lettuce, tomato, avocado, salsa, yogurt, and cheese. Serve immediately.

Yield:

6 tostadas

Nutrition Information (per toastada):

259 calories; 11.8 g fat; 114 mg cholesterol; 307 mg sodium; 18.7 g carbohydrate; 2.8 g fiber; 20.7 g protein

Cook's Comment:

I love cooking with shrimp because they cook so quickly and are ideal for a meal that's ready in minutes. These tostadas take 15 minutes to cook from start to finish, including the prep time. A perfect meal for someone looking for big flavor, but is short on time!

 To make this recipe gluten-free, use corn tostadas.

Slow-Cooked Pork Carnitas Tacos

3.5 lbs boneless, center-cut pork loin, lean, with all visible fat removed

1 teaspoon salt

¾ teaspoon black pepper

1 tablespoon olive oil

6 cloves garlic, cut into quarters

2 tablespoons cumin

2 teaspoons adobo seasoning

2 teaspoons garlic powder

1¼ cups low-sodium chicken broth

6 chipotle peppers in adobo sauce, chopped

2 bay leaves

Directions:

Season pork with salt and pepper. In a large skillet over medium-high heat, heat olive oil. Once hot, add pork, and brown on all sides for approximately 10 minutes. Remove from heat, and allow to cool.

With a sharp knife, insert blade into pork; cut small holes, and insert garlic. Season pork with spices; rub to coat well.

Pour chicken broth in slow cooker. Add bay leaves and chipotle peppers. Place pork in slow cooker, and cover. Cook low 9–12 hours.

After cooking, shred pork using two forks, and combine well with the juices that accumulated at the bottom. Remove bay leaves.

Yield:

10 servings (5 oz. each)

Nutrition Information (per serving):

216 calories; 8.5 g fat; 91 mg cholesterol; 585 mg sodium; 2.5 g carbohydrate; 0.2 g fiber; 31.3 g protein

Nutrition Note:

Traditional carnitas are made with pork shoulder or pork butt, both of which contain plenty of fat and are subsequently high in calories and saturated fat. Using a slow-cooking method allows for a leaner cut of meat that still will fall apart and shred effortlessly.

Halibut with Cold Cucumber Salad

4 (5 oz.) halibut filets
¼ teaspoon salt and pepper, divided
1 cucumber, seeded and diced
1 Roma tomato, seeded and diced

3 tablespoons red onion, chopped
1 tablespoon red wine vinegar
1 tablespoon olive oil

Directions:

Preheat oven to 350°F. Spray baking dish with nonstick cooking spray.

Arrange halibut on the baking sheet, and season with a pinch of salt and pepper. Bake 10–12 minutes.

Meanwhile, combine cucumber, tomato, onion, vinegar, and oil in a small bowl. Season with a pinch of salt and pepper.

Serve halibut hot with cucumber salad over top.

Yield:

4 servings (5 oz. fish with approximately ⅓ cup cucumber salad)

Nutrition Information (per serving):

211 calories; 7 g fat; 45 mg cholesterol; 147 mg sodium; 5.8 g carbohydrate; 1.3 g fiber; 30.8 g protein

Cook's Comment:

Using different textures in dishes is a technique in and of itself. I often find that people don't enjoy seafood because of the tender, limp consistency. While halibut prices are on the higher side, the consistency of the fish is meaty. Topping with a cucumber salad adds crunch and great texture variation. This dish is perfect for summer!

Coconut Shrimp and Chickpea Curry

1½ cups dry brown basmati rice

1 tablespoon extra-virgin olive oil

1 yellow onion, chopped

1 teaspoon black pepper

1 tablespoon (about a 1-inch piece) fresh
   ginger, minced

½ teaspoon salt

2 garlic cloves, peeled and finely minced

2 teaspoons ground coriander

½ teaspoon turmeric

⅛ teaspoon cayenne

1½ teaspoons curry powder

1 (14.5-oz.) can no-salt-added diced tomatoes, undrained

1 lb large shrimp, peeled and deveined

1 (15-oz.) can chickpeas, drained and rinsed

1 can light coconut milk

½ cup fresh cilantro, chopped

Directions:

In a large saucepan, bring 3 cups water to a boil. Stir in rice; return to a boil. Reduce heat to low, and cover. Cook 20–30 minutes, according to package directions.

Meanwhile, in a medium-sized stockpot, heat oil over medium-high heat until hot. Add onion, and cook 2–3 minutes. Stir in pepper, ginger, salt, garlic, coriander, turmeric, and curry powder. Continue cooking, stirring often, until onion is soft and translucent, approximately 5 minutes.

Add undrained tomatoes to the pot, and cook, stirring constantly, for approximately 1 minute. Add coconut milk, and bring to a simmer. Simmer 5–6 minutes, stirring often.

Add shrimp and chickpeas; cook until shrimp are pink and curled, approximately 3–4 minutes. Stir in cilantro. Serve over hot, cooked rice.

Yield:

6 servings (about 1 cup rice and 1 cup curry)

Nutrition Information (per serving):

413 calories; 11.0 g fat; 100 mg cholesterol; 460 mg sodium; 55.7 g carbohydrate; 7.0 g fiber; 23.5 g protein

Nutrition Note:

I thoroughly enjoy making Indian food at home. Once you have your supply of spices, you'll be amazed at the flavors you can produce. Thanks to these spices, Indian food is also low in calories and fat . . . especially when you use items such as low-fat coconut milk (coconut milk is a staple in Indian and Thai cuisines). The smell of curry wafting through the house is nearly as good as the meal!

Meat-Free Mains

Caprese Quinoa Patties
with Balsamic Ricotta

Tomato Tart

Black Bean and Rice
Stuffed Peppers

Tofu and Vegetables in Spicy
Peanut Sauce

Kung Pao Tofu

Gruyére Risotto with Asparagus
and Mushrooms

Baked Potato Skins Veggie Pizzas

Lentil Tacos

Baked Falafel

Spinach, Marinated Mushroom,
and Artichoke Stuffed Portabellos

Quinoa Black Bean Burrito Bowls

Caprese Quinoa Patties with Balsamic Ricotta

1 cup dry quinoa
¼ cup red onion, finely diced
¼ teaspoon kosher salt
¼ teaspoon black pepper
3 large eggs, beaten
½ cup (2 oz.) mozzarella, finely shredded
¾ cup bread crumbs
2 oz. soft goat cheese, crumbled

¼ cup low-fat ricotta
1 teaspoon balsamic vinegar
2 tablespoons olive oil for pan-frying, divided

Balsamic Ricotta:

½ cup low-fat ricotta
2 tablespoons balsamic vinegar

Directions:

Bring 2 cups water to a boil in a medium-sized saucepan. Add quinoa, stir, and return to a boil. Cover and simmer approximately 12 minutes. Remove from heat, and allow to steam, with lid on, 15 minutes. Fluff with a fork.

In a medium-sized bowl, combine cooked quinoa with onion, salt, and pepper. Stir in remaining quinoa patty ingredients (through vinegar) and form into 8 patties.

Heat 1 tablespoon oil in a large skillet over medium heat. Add 4 patties, and cook 6–8 minutes or until golden brown. Flip, and cook an additional 2–3 minutes until browned. Transfer to a plate lined with paper towels to absorb excess oil. Repeat with remaining oil and patties.

While patties cook, combine ricotta and balsamic vinegar.

Yield:

8 patties (about 3½ inches in diameter, 1-inch thick) with 1 tablespoon balsamic ricotta

Nutrition Information (per patty):

245 calories; 10.8 g fat; 83 mg cholesterol; 274 mg sodium; 24.8 g carbohydrate; 2.0 g fiber; 11.8 g protein

Cook's Comment:

Vegetarian patties that are pan-fried tend to lose moisture quickly, and the result is tough and dry. But not these! With egg, goat cheese, and ricotta, these quinoa patties pack flavor and excellent texture and consistency. I love to make extra quinoa for other dishes and use the excess to make these the following night!

Use gluten-free bread crumbs to create a gluten-free meal!

Tomato Tart

1¼ cups whole-wheat pastry flour

1 teaspoon sugar

½ teaspoon salt

6 tablespoons cold unsalted butter, cut into small pieces

1 large egg

1 teaspoon ice water, plus more if needed

1 teaspoon extra-virgin olive oil

3 large tomatoes, sliced thick

12 oz. fresh mozzarella, sliced thick

¼ cup basil, chopped

Directions:

Combine flour, sugar, and salt in a food processor, and pulse to combine. Add butter, and pulse several times until flour resembles coarse crumbs. Beat the egg with the ice water, and pour it into the food processor; pulse a few moments until dough comes together into a ball, adding more water if needed.

Remove dough from the processor, and flatten into a disc. Wrap dough in plastic wrap, and refrigerate 2–3 hours.

Preheat oven to 400°F.

When dough is chilled, roll it out into a round circle approximately ¼-inch thick and at least 12 inches in diameter. Spray a 10-inch tart pan with nonstick cooking spray, and transfer dough to the pan. Using a fork, poke several holes into bottom of crust, and brush with olive oil. Par-bake the crust 10–15 minutes, until beginning to brown.

Layer tomatoes and mozzarella in the tart. Bake for approximately 18–20 minutes until cheese is melted. Remove from oven, and allow to cool slightly before serving. Garnish with basil.

Yield:

8 slices

Nutrition Information (per slice):

257 calories; 16.1 g fat; 46 mg cholesterol; 190 mg sodium; 16.9 g carbohydrate; 2.8 g fiber; 10.4 g protein

Nutrition Note:

It's OK to use butter! Just keep your portions in check. I used to avoid recipes calling for butter, but I had never stopped to do the math. This recipe, for example, has 6 tablespoons of butter, but it serves 8 portions. That equals less than 1 tablespoon of butter per portion . . . probably less than what people smear on their dinner rolls!

Black Bean and Rice Stuffed Peppers

¼ cup uncooked brown rice

2 large red or green bell peppers, halved and seeded

2 teaspoons extra-virgin olive oil

½ onion, chopped

2 garlic cloves, minced

1 (15-oz.) can black beans, drained and rinsed

⅓ cup corn (frozen or fresh)

Pinch of cayenne pepper

½ tablespoon chili powder

½ teaspoon paprika

½ teaspoon oregano

1 teaspoon cumin

Squeeze of lime juice

⅓ cup part-skim Mexican-blend shredded cheese

¼ cup cilantro, roughly chopped

Nutrition Note:

By draining and rinsing canned beans, you get rid of at least 40 percent of the sodium. Be sure to do so when using canned beans in recipes!

Directions:

Turn broiler to 550°F. Place halved and cleaned bell peppers onto a baking sheet lined with tinfoil or parchment, skin-side up. Broil 4–6 minutes, until blackened. Place in airtight container or zip-top bag, and let sit 10 minutes. When cool enough to handle, peel off skin or scrape skin with a knife blade to remove.

Meanwhile, cook rice according to package directions.

Preheat oven to 375°F.

Heat olive oil in large skillet over medium-high heat. Add onion, and cook until tender, approximately 3 minutes. Add garlic, and cook 30 seconds, until fragrant. Stir in beans, and reduce heat to low. Stir in cooked rice, corn, and all seasonings and lime juice (optional). Warm through, approximately 1–2 minutes.

Return pepper halves to lined baking sheet. Stuff each pepper half with rice and bean mixture. Top with cheese, and bake for 12–15 minutes. Garnish with cilantro. Serve immediately.

Yield:

4 servings (½ stuffed pepper each)

Nutrition Information (per serving):

228 calories; 5.8 g fat; 6 mg cholesterol; 275 mg sodium; 35.3 g carbohydrate; 9 g fiber; 11.3 g protein

Tofu and Vegetables in Spicy Peanut Sauce

1 block extra-firm tofu, drained and cubed
1 head (approximately 5 cups) broccoli florets
1 cup carrots, peeled, and sliced into thin, 1-inch pieces
1 bell pepper, sliced into 2-inch pieces
⅓ cup nut butter (almond, peanut, etc.)
1-inch piece ginger, peeled and diced

3 cloves garlic, chopped
3 tablespoons low-sodium soy sauce
2 tablespoons sugar
1 tablespoon toasted sesame oil
2 tablespoons seasoned rice vinegar
1 teaspoon red pepper flakes (more or less for spice preference)

Directions:

Preheat oven to 475°F.

Spray a lined baking sheet with olive oil. Arrange tofu cubes in a single layer. Spray cubes with olive oil, and bake 30 minutes.

In a food processor or blender, mix nut butter, ginger, garlic, soy sauce, sugar, oil, vinegar, and red pepper flakes. Set aside.

5 minutes before tofu is finished, steam vegetables by splashing them with 1–2 tablespoons water and microwaving 4–5 minutes in a large glass casserole dish fitted with a lid. Drain in a colander, and return to casserole dish. Add tofu and sauce; toss to combine. Serve immediately with rice or grain of choice, if desired.

Yield:

4 servings (about 1½ cups vegetables and tofu each)

Nutrition Information (per serving):

354 calories; 20.0 g fat; 0 mg cholesterol; 568 mg sodium; 28.8 g carbohydrate; 6.3 g fiber; 19.8 g protein

Nutrition Note:

Peanut sauces are great go-to options for quick meals, because they can go on absolutely anything and still taste great. Feel free to swap in your favorite protein, but I love this with tofu. The vegetables soak up the peanut sauce, and if you like things spicy, you easily can bump up the red pepper flakes to suit your preferences!

Kung Pao Tofu

12 oz. extra-firm tofu, drained and cubed

⅓ cup roasted peanuts

1 tablespoon coconut oil

½ teaspoon crushed red pepper flakes, or
more to taste

1 red bell pepper, sliced into strips

1 cup mushrooms, sliced

2–3 green onions, sliced and divided

1 tablespoon seasoned rice vinegar

2 tablespoons gluten-free soy sauce

2 garlic cloves, minced

1-inch piece fresh ginger, peeled and grated

Directions:

Preheat oven to 425°F. Line a baking sheet with tinfoil, and spray with nonstick cooking spray. Arrange tofu on the baking sheet, and lightly mist with oil. Bake 30 minutes, turning cubes after 15 minutes.

Heat coconut oil in a wok over medium-high heat. Add peanuts and red pepper flakes, and cook 2–3 minutes, stirring frequently. Add tofu and stir.

Add bell pepper and mushrooms, and cook another 1–2 minutes.

Add half of green onions, vinegar, soy sauce, garlic, and ginger. Reduce heat, and allow sauce to thicken 2–3 minutes. Serve over cooked brown rice, if desired, and top with remaining green onions.

Yield:

3 servings (about 1¼ cups each)

Nutrition Information (per serving):

268 calories; 16 g fat; 0 mg cholesterol; 532 mg sodium; 11.3 g carbohydrate; 4.7 g fiber; 16.7 g protein

Cook's Comment:

Tofu is one of my favorite meat alternatives. It's affordable and so versatile in recipes. I enjoy tofu best when it has been baked so that it takes on a firm exterior with a soft, chewy interior. Tofu will take on the flavors it is served with, which is exactly why this meal is sure to go over well even with the tofu novice!

Gruyére Risotto with Asparagus and Mushrooms

4 cups low-sodium vegetable broth

1 tablespoon olive oil

1 bunch (1 lb) asparagus, with tough ends removed and chopped into 2-inch pieces

2 cups (8 oz.) mushrooms, washed and sliced

1 tablespoon butter

3 small shallots, chopped

3 garlic cloves, minced

1 cup arborio rice, dry

1½ cups (6 oz.) Gruyére cheese, shredded

¼ cup lemon juice (juice from 1–2 lemons)

Directions:

In a saucepan over low heat, warm vegetable stock. Keep warm.

Meanwhile, heat olive oil over medium-high heat in a large pan, and sauté asparagus and mushrooms until tender, approximately 8–10 minutes. Transfer mushrooms and asparagus to a plate or bowl; set aside.

Melt butter over medium-high heat in the same skillet. Sauté shallots 2–3 minutes or until tender; add garlic, and sauté for an additional minute. Add rice, and stir until well-coated and translucent. Reduce heat to medium, and stir in 1 cup vegetable broth. Simmer, stirring occasionally, until broth has been absorbed; add another cup, and continue in this way until all vegetable broth has been absorbed, for approximately 30 minutes.

Stir in Gruyére cheese, lemon juice, and salt, and simmer an additional 5 minutes or until desired consistency is reached. Stir in asparagus and mushrooms to heat through.

Yield:

5 servings (about 1 heaping cup each)

Nutrition Information (1 heaping cup):

356 calories, 16.6 g fat, 30 mg cholesterol; 320 mg sodium; 37.2 g carbohydrate; 2.2 g fiber, 12.8 g protein

Fun Fact:

This is probably my husband's most favorite meal to date. He praised this for its Italian authenticity, and the flavors are absolutely unmatched. I refer to risotto as perfect date food—food doesn't get more romantic than this!

Baked Potato Skins Veggie Pizzas

4 medium russet potatoes, scrubbed
Cooking spray
¼ teaspoon salt
1 cup low-sodium tomato
   sauce

1¼ cups part-skim mozzarella cheese,
   shredded
¼ bell pepper, thinly sliced
Italian seasoning, to taste
Crushed red pepper flakes, to taste

Directions:

Preheat oven to 400°F.

Place potatoes on a large baking tray. Bake potatoes 45–50 minutes or until softened. Remove from oven, and let potatoes cool slightly.

Cut each potato in half, and scoop out flesh, leaving approximately ¼-inch of potato skin. Lightly spray potato skins with cooking spray, and season with salt. Bake 15 minutes, flipping potato skins halfway through.

Fill each skin with about 2 tablespoons tomato sauce, and top with cheese and bell pepper. Bake 15–16 minutes or until cheese has melted. Allow to cook 5 minutes, and serve warm.

Yield:

8 potato-skin pizzas

Nutrition Information (per skin):

101 calories; 3 g fat; 9 mg cholesterol; 190 mg sodium; 11.9 g carbohydrate; 1.6 g fiber; 7 g protein

Fun Fact:

My husband's favorite food is pizza. He would eat it at every meal if I let him. Finding new ways to enjoy his favorites—and mine—with added nutrition is always a perk! Replacing a buttery crust made with all-purpose flour for a fiber- and nutrient-packed potato skin is perfect! These potato-skin pizzas are perfect for kids, game day, or a lighter meal. Get creative with the toppings by encouraging kids to see how many colors they can add to their pizzas.

Lentil Tacos

1 teaspoon extra-virgin olive oil

½ yellow onion, finely chopped

1 garlic clove, minced

1 cup dried lentils, rinsed

1 tablespoon chili powder

2 teaspoons ground cumin

1 teaspoon dried oregano

2½ cups low-sodium vegetable broth

2 cups lettuce, shredded

1 large tomato, diced

1 avocado, sliced

⅔ cup part-skim cheddar cheese, shredded

⅔ cup nonfat plain Greek yogurt

⅔ cup salsa

10 (6-inch) flour tortillas

Directions:

In a nonstick saucepan, heat oil until hot. Add onion and garlic, and sauté until tender.

Add lentils, chili powder, cumin, and oregano; cook and stir 1 minute. Add broth; bring to a boil. Reduce heat; cover and simmer 25–30 minutes or until lentils are tender. Uncover; cook 6–8 minutes or until mixture is thickened. Mash lentils by smashing them against sides of saucepan with the back of a spoon.

To make tacos, layer approximately ¼ cup lentils into each of 10 tortillas. Top with a pinch of lettuce, spoonful of tomato, avocado slice, and 1 tablespoon cheese, salsa, and Greek yogurt.

Yield:

5 servings (2 tacos each)

Nutrition Information (per serving):

425 calories; 11.2 g fat; 10 mg cholesterol; 799 mg sodium; 59.2 g carbohydrate; 17.6 g fiber; 22.4 g protein

Nutrition Note:

Legumes, such as lentils, rarely are consumed in the traditional American diet, but they are plentiful in ethnic cuisines, such as Indian food. Low in calories and high in fiber and protein, lentils are a great go-to for vegetarian main dishes.

 Looking for a gluten-free snack? Use corn tortillas.

Baked Falafel

1 cup dried garbanzo beans
½ large onion, roughly chopped (about 1 cup)
2 tablespoons fresh parsley
2 tablespoons fresh cilantro

1 teaspoon salt
4 cloves garlic
¾ teaspoon cumin
1 teaspoon baking powder
6 tablespoons all-purpose flour

Directions:

Soak beans overnight in plenty of water.

The next day, put garbanzo beans and onion in the food processor, and pulse to roughly chop. Next, add remaining ingredients, and pulse until combined. Refrigerate mixture for 30 minutes, up to several hours.

After mixture is chilled, preheat oven to 375°F.

Form garbanzo bean mixture into 25 walnut-sized balls. Place on a greased baking sheet, and bake 25–30 minutes. Increase oven temperature to a 500°F broil. Broil falafel 3–5 minutes (or longer) until tops are golden brown.

Serve with pita, cucumbers, tomato, and either hummus or a tahini yogurt sauce.

Yield:

15 falafel

Nutrition Information (per falafel):

43 calories; 0.53 g fat; 0 mg cholesterol; 150 mg sodium; 8.7 g carbohydrate; 1.7 g fiber; 2.3 g protein

Fun Fact:

My first job was in a Middle Eastern restaurant. That summer, I probably ate my body weight in falafel. I love the stuff! Rather than frying, this falafel recipe is baked and healthful. The herbs and cumin work *magic* in this recipe. You'll never head out for falafel again. Serve this with hummus, cucumber, and tomato . . . at least, that's how I love it best! Pita, too!

Spinach, Marinated Mushroom, and Artichoke Stuffed Portobellos

Olive oil spray

4 large portobello mushroom caps

¼ teaspoon salt and freshly ground black pepper, to taste

4 oz. reduced-fat cream cheese, at room temperature

3 tablespoons low-fat olive oil-based mayonnaise

3 cloves garlic, minced, divided

1½ teaspoons dried Italian seasoning

10 oz. froz.en chopped spinach, thawed and squeezed dry

6 oz. marinated mushrooms, drained and roughly chopped

6 oz. marinated artichoke hearts, drained and roughly chopped

1 tablespoon olive oil

⅓ cup coarse panko bread crumbs

¼ cup (1 oz.) Parmesan or Parmigiano-Reggiano cheese, finely grated

Directions:

Preheat oven to 450°F.

Scrape gills and stem from inside the mushroom caps. Set mushroom caps on a baking pan, gill-side up, and spray with olive oil; season with salt and pepper. Bake 10 minutes.

Meanwhile, prepare filling. Combine cream cheese, mayonnaise, garlic, ½ teaspoon of Italian seasoning, and spinach in a medium-sized. Stir until evenly blended. Gently stir in marinated mushrooms and artichokes. Spoon filling mixture into mushroom caps.

In another small bowl, combine olive oil with bread crumbs, cheese, and remaining 1 teaspoon Italian seasoning with a fork. Sprinkle bread-crumb mixture over the top of each mushroom. Bake for an additional 10 minutes or until golden and warmed through. Serve immediately.

Yield:

4 large mushroom caps

Nutrition Information (per cap):

255 calories; 17.8 g fat; 25 mg cholesterol; 488 mg sodium; 15.8 g carbohydrate; 4.0 g fiber; 12.3 g protein

Nutrition Note:

Using reduced-fat or light ingredients can add up to huge calorie and fat savings. This recipe uses cream cheese and mayonnaise for a creamy result . . . but there's no reason to feel guilty. One of these stuffed portobellos makes for a perfect summer meal that's on the lighter side. Enjoy with a salad, or share a second with someone you love!

Use gluten-free bread crumbs if you're planning on serving a gluten-free meal!

Quinoa Black Bean Burrito Bowls

2 cups water
1 cup uncooked quinoa
1 tablespoon olive oil
½ onion, chopped
2 cloves garlic, minced
1 can black beans, drained and rinsed
½ cup cilantro, chopped
2 teaspoons chili powder

Pinch of cayenne
¼ cup fresh lime juice (from 1–2 limes), divided
2 tomatoes, diced
¼ cup nonfat plain Greek yogurt
½ cup 2% cheddar cheese, shredded
½ avocado, pitted and diced
¼ cup salsa

Directions:

Heat water in a saucepan and bring to a boil. Add quinoa, stir, and return to a boil. Lower heat, cover, and simmer approximately 15–20 minutes. Remove from heat, and allow to steam 10–15 minutes.

Meanwhile, heat olive oil in a medium-sized skillet over medium-high heat. Add onions, and cook until softened. Add garlic, and cook 1 minute. Add black beans, half of cilantro, chili powder, cayenne, and 2 tablespoons lime juice. Reduce heat to low.

When quinoa is fully cooked, remove from heat and fluff with a fork. Stir in remaining cilantro and remaining lime juice. To assemble bowls, divide quinoa among three bowls. Top with black beans, tomatoes, yogurt, cheese, avocado, and salsa. Serve warm.

Yield:

3 servings

Nutrition Information (per serving):

549 calories; 19 g fat; 13 mg cholesterol; 456 mg sodium; 77 g carbohydrate; 16 g fiber; 24.7 g protein

Nutrition Note:

Using quinoa is a gluten-free option that is high in fiber and protein, which makes it perfect for vegetarian and vegan fare. While quinoa is gaining popularity, it can be found in major retailers near the gluten-free or healthful foods sections.

You easily can make this recipe for your vegan and dairy-free friends. Just skip the cheese!

Carb Lovers

Roasted Red Pepper and Goat
Cheese Pasta

Cajun Chicken Pasta

Light Fettuccine Alfredo

Skillet BBQ Chicken Pasta

Turkey Goulash

Greek Orzo

Pasta and Zucchini in Basil Cream
with Grilled Chicken

Pasta with Brussels Sprouts,
Gorgonzola, and Pecans

Butternut Squash Mac and Cheese

Roasted Red Pepper and Goat Cheese Pasta

10 oz. dry whole-wheat fettuccine or linguine

15-oz. can fire-roasted diced tomatoes

5 oz. goat cheese

12-oz. jar roasted red pepper, drained

1 tablespoon extra-virgin olive oil

2 small zucchini, sliced into ¼-inch half moons

Salt and pepper, to taste

Directions:

Bring a pot of lightly salted water to a rolling boil; add pasta, and cook 9–11 minutes until al dente. Drain, and set aside.

Meanwhile, combine tomatoes, goat cheese, and peppers in a blender or food processor; process until smooth.

In a large saucepan, heat olive oil. Add zucchini, salt, and pepper to taste, and sauté 2–3 minutes until zucchini begins to soften and brown. Add goat cheese sauce to zucchini, and simmer 6–7 minutes or until heated through.

Combine pasta and sauce in a large bowl, and serve hot.

Yield:

4 servings (approximately 1½ cups each)

Nutrition Information (per serving):

424 calories; 13.8 g fat; 19 mg cholesterol; 266 mg sodium; 62.8 g carbohydrate; 11 g fiber; 15.5 g protein

Fun Fact:

This recipe came about when I didn't want to go grocery shopping. I grabbed 3 flavor-packed ingredients—roasted red peppers, goat cheese, and fire-roasted tomatoes—blended them together, and came up with a pasta sauce you will absolutely love. Get creative in the kitchen. You never know what you'll come up with!

Cajun Chicken Pasta

10 oz. whole-wheat linguine

1 lb boneless, skinless chicken breasts

4 teaspoons Cajun seasoning

1 tablespoon extra-virgin olive oil

1 red bell pepper, sliced into strips

1 green bell pepper, sliced into strips

1 large yellow onion, halved and thinly sliced

3 garlic cloves, minced

1½ cups half-and-half

1 teaspoon dried basil

Directions:

Bring a large pot of water to a boil. Add pasta, and cook 8–10 minutes or until al dente; drain, and set aside.

Meanwhile, cut chicken breasts into thin strips, and season with 2 teaspoons Cajun seasoning. In a large skillet over medium heat, sauté chicken in olive oil 4–5 minutes or until no longer pink.

Add onion, and sauté 1–2 minutes. Add garlic, and sauté an additional minute. Add red and green bell peppers. Sauté 2–3 minutes, until peppers are slightly tender.

Add half-and-half and basil; bring to a boil. Add cooked linguine, tossing to allow half-and-half to cook into al-dente pasta. Add remaining 2 teaspoons Cajun seasoning.

Yield:

6 servings (approximately 1½ cups each)

Nutrition Information (per serving):

364 calories; 10.3 g fat; 57 mg cholesterol; 437 mg sodium; 42.4 g carbohydrate; 6.5 g fiber; 24.2 g protein

Shopping Tip:

Cajun seasoning is actually easy to find, and after you try it in this recipe, you'll fall in love. I love the heat with the smoky flavors—the Cajun seasoning is what takes the everyday onions and bell peppers in this recipe to a new level.

Light Fettuccine Alfredo

8 oz. dry fettuccine

1 tablespoon unsalted butter

2 garlic cloves, minced

1 tablespoon all-purpose flour

1⅓ cups 1% low-fat milk

¾ cup (3 oz.) Parmesan cheese, finely
  shredded

2 oz. low-fat cream cheese

¼ teaspoon salt

2 teaspoons flat-leaf parsley, chopped

Freshly ground black pepper, to taste

Nutrition Note:

Alfredo sauce is a favorite among many because it is *very* rich and creamy. The goal of this dish is to closely replicate Alfredo with a *fraction* of the calories and fat. There's no heavy cream in this recipe . . . and, you won't even miss it!

Directions:

Heat 2–3 quarts of water in a large pot. Once boiling, add fettuccine, and cool until al dente, stirring occasionally.

Meanwhile, melt butter in a saucepan over medium heat. Add garlic, and cook just until fragrant, about 30 seconds, stirring frequently. Whisk in flour, then gradually whisk in milk, stirring constantly until mixture thickens, approximately 3–4 minutes. Add Parmesan cream cheese, and salt, stirring until cheeses melt.

Add hot, drained pasta, and toss to distribute. Serve with a sprinkle of parsley and black pepper, if desired.

Yield:

4 servings (1 heaping cup each)

Nutrition Information (per serving):

388 calories; 13.5 g fat; 32 mg cholesterol; 379 mg sodium; 2 g fiber; 17.8 g protein

Skillet BBQ Chicken Pasta

1 teaspoon extra-virgin olive oil

1 lb boneless, skinless chicken breasts, cut into bite-sized chunks

1 red onion, diced

2 cups water

2 cups low-sodium chicken broth

12 oz. whole-wheat penne pasta

½ cup barbecue sauce

⅓ cup 2% plain Greek yogurt

⅓ cup 2% mozzarella cheese, shredded

⅓ cup 2% sharp cheddar cheese, shredded

Cook's Comment:

This is truly a one-pot meal—you've got to love it! This is comfort food at its finest without any of the guilt. Whole-wheat pasta and reduced-fat dairy make this recipe sure to please!

Directions:

In a large 12-inch nonstick skillet, heat olive oil over medium heat. When hot, add chicken and onions, and sauté, stirring occasionally, until chicken is browned and cooked through. Transfer chicken and onions to a plate, and set aside.

In the same skillet, add water, chicken broth, penne, and salt. Bring to a boil, and simmer 12–15 minutes, until liquid is almost absorbed, pasta is tender, and mixture is thick and syrupy. Stir in barbecue sauce and Greek yogurt. Once mixed, add reserved chicken, onions, and shredded cheese. Stir to combine, and cook until everything is heated through.

Serve immediately, and garnish with additional red or green onions.

Yield:

6 servings (about 1⅓ cups each)

Nutrition Information (per serving):

375 calories; 4.8 g fat; 45 mg cholesterol; 479 mg sodium; 50.8 g carbohydrate; 4.8 g fiber; 32.5 g protein

Turkey Goulash

1 teaspoon olive oil

1 lb ground turkey breast

1 onion, diced

2 garlic cloves, minced

2 cups water

1 (15-oz.) can no-salt-added tomato sauce

1 (15-oz.) can no-salt-added diced tomatoes

1½ teaspoons Italian seasoning

1 tablespoon low-sodium soy sauce

1 bay leaf

¼ teaspoon black pepper

2 cups whole-wheat elbow macaroni

Directions:

Heat olive oil in a Dutch oven over medium-high heat.

Sauté onion 2–3 minutes until softened; add garlic, and sauté until fragrant, approximately 1 minute. Add turkey, and cook until no longer pink, breaking up meat with a wooden spoon.

Add water, tomato sauce, diced tomatoes, Italian seasoning, soy sauce, bay leaf, and black pepper. Bring to a boil; add pasta, and stir. Cover, and reduce heat to low; cook 20 minutes or until pasta is al dente. Remove bay leaf before serving. Serve hot.

Yield:

7 servings (approximately 1½ cups each)

Nutrition Information (per serving):

227 calories; 1.7 g fat; 28 mg cholesterol; 513 mg sodium; 30.8 g carbohydrate; 4.9 g fiber; 22.3 g protein

Fun Fact:

When I moved to Tulsa, I never had heard of goulash—it's not a dish that is commonly served in the Chicagoland region. When I counseled patients, so many of them mentioned goulash in their food recalls. I would ask, "What goes into your goulash recipe?" I would hear just about any ingredient under the sun, but it seemed that ground beef, pasta, and tomatoes were the staples. This goulash recipe is made with the help of so many of my patients from Oklahoma . . . with a healthful spin.

Greek Orzo

1 cup dry orzo

Juice of ½ lemon

3 tablespoons dry white wine

2 tablespoons olive oil

¼ teaspoon salt

¼ teaspoon pepper

1 lb raw shrimp, peeled and deveined

1 tablespoon fresh oregano, chopped, or
   1 teaspoon dried oregano

2 tomatoes, roughly chopped

¼ cup kalamata olives (about 14), pitted and
   halved

⅓ cup feta cheese, crumbled

¼ cup parsley, chopped

Directions:

In a large saucepan, bring 1 quart water to a rolling boil. Add orzo, and stir. Cook orzo 7–8 minutes until al dente. Drain, and set aside.

Meanwhile, combine lemon juice, wine, oil, salt, and pepper in a small bowl. Toss ½ of lemon juice mixture with shrimp in a medium-sized bowl. Reserve remaining lemon juice mixture.

Return saucepan to medium heat, and add shrimp (and any unabsorbed lemon juice mixture). Cook shrimp 2–3 minutes. Add oregano and tomatoes; cook an additional 2–3 minutes.

Add cooked orzo to the saucepan, along with reserved lemon juice mixture. Stir to combine. Add olives, and cook an additional 1–2 minutes or until orzo absorbs most liquid. Top with feta and parsley, and serve immediately.

Yield:

4 servings (approximately 1½ cups each)

Nutrition Information (per serving):

438 calories; 16.8 g fat; 153 mg cholesterol; 632 mg sodium; 39.5 g carbohydrate; 3.8 g fiber; 31.8 g protein

Cook's Comment:

There's nothing extraordinary about any of the ingredients . . . but together, they are absolutely delicious. This one-pot meal is packed with flavor. If you buy large shrimp, this meal will feel like a real treat! This meal is a favorite, for sure!

Pasta and Zucchini in Basil Cream with Grilled Chicken

1 lb chicken, cut into strips
12 oz. whole-wheat pasta
2 zucchini, sliced
2 tablespoons unsalted butter
2 tablespoons all-purpose flour

1½ cups 2% milk
2 garlic cloves, minced
½ cup basil leaves, minced
½ teaspoon salt and pepper, to taste

Directions:

Preheat grill to medium heat. Add chicken strips, and grill 4–5 minutes; flip and grill an additional 2–3 minutes.

Meanwhile, bring a large pot of water to a rolling boil. Add pasta, and stir. Cook 10 minutes. Add zucchini to pasta, and cook an additional 3–5 minutes. Strain, and set aside.

In a small saucepan, melt butter over medium-high heat. Whisk in flour, whisking continuously for 1–2 minutes; whisk in milk. Bring to a simmer, whisking occasionally. Once thickened, about 6–8 minutes, add garlic and basil. Continue simmering to thicken an additional 2–3 minutes. Season with salt and pepper.

Combine pasta and sauce; toss. Serve topped with chicken.

Yield:

6 servings (1⅓ cups pasta and zucchini with 2½ oz. chicken)

Nutrition Information (per serving):

366 calories; 8.0 g fat; 42 mg cholesterol; 258 mg sodium; 48.3 g carbohydrate; 6.8 g fiber; 27.5 g protein

Cook's Comment:

When you start a sauce with butter and flour, it's called a roux. Using a bit of fat in making a roux will produce a thick and creamy sauce that will work exceptionally well with low-fat milk. Using low-fat instead of fat-free milk adds flavor and creaminess with few added calories or additional fat. The basil in this cream sauce is subtle and perfectly suited for those who prefer milder flavors. Don't forget the salt—the sauce will need it!

Pasta with Brussels Sprouts, Gorgonzola, and Pecans

4 cups (20 oz.) Brussels sprouts, thinly sliced
to shred
½ teaspoon salt and black pepper, to taste
2 teaspoons extra-virgin olive oil
13.25 oz. whole-wheat shells or orecchiette
1½ tablespoons unsalted butter

½ cup (2 oz.) chopped pecans, coarsely
4 cloves garlic, minced
½ cup half-and-half
¾ cup 2% milk
¾ cup (3 oz.) Gorgonzola, crumbled

Cook's Comment:

This is a great fall recipe—Brussels sprouts are in season, and the cream sauce is a guilt-free treat. The portion size of this recipe is plentiful, because the Brussels sprouts help stretch the pasta. Using vegetables in pasta is a great way to enjoy pasta while keeping calories and carbohydrates in check. Opt for whole-wheat pastas when available; the fiber content is extremely high.

Directions:

Preheat oven to 500°F.

Line a baking sheet with tinfoil, and spray with nonstick cooking spray. Toss Brussels sprouts with olive oil, and season with salt and pepper. Arrange Brussels sprouts in a single layer on the baking sheet, and bake 12–15 minutes, tossing halfway through.

Meanwhile, fill a large pot with 3 quarts water; bring to a boil over high heat. Once boiling, add pasta, and cook 9–11 minutes until al dente; drain, and set aside.

In a skillet over medium heat, melt ½ tablespoon butter. Add pecans, cooking until pecans are toasted and butter is browned, approximately 3 minutes; remove pecans with a slotted spoon, and place on a plate. In the same skillet, melt remaining tablespoon butter. Cook garlic until softened, another 3 minutes, still stirring frequently. Add half-and-half and milk, and bring to a simmer. Remove from heat, and add ¾ cup Gorgonzola, stirring until melted.

In a serving bowl, toss pasta, pecans, Brussels sprouts, and Gorgonzola cream sauce. Serve immediately.

Yield:

7 servings (approximately 1½ cups each)

Nutrition Information (per serving):

378 calories; 17.6 g fat; 19 mg cholesterol; 358 mg sodium; 47.0 g carbohydrate; 7.9 g fiber; 12.3 g protein

Butternut Squash Mac and Cheese

3½ cups cubed, peeled butternut squash
  (about one 1-lb squash)
1¼ cups fat-free, low-sodium vegetable
  broth
2 garlic cloves, chopped
1½ cups fat-free milk
1 lb uncooked whole-wheat pasta (such as
  penne or rotini)

¼ teaspoon kosher salt
½ teaspoon freshly ground black pepper
2 tablespoons fat-free Greek yogurt
1¼ cups (5 oz.) Gruyére cheese, shredded
1 cup (4 oz.) pecorino Romano cheese, grated
¼ cup (1 oz.) Parmigiano-Reggiano cheese,
  grated

Nutrition Note:

Using broth and fat-free milk as the base of the cheese sauce in this macaroni and cheese makes for the saving of calories and fat. Using bold cheeses, such as Gruyére and pecorino Romano compliment the sweet butternut squash. You wouldn't think this would work . . . but it is so good!

Directions:

Combine squash, broth, garlic, and milk in a medium-sized saucepan; bring to a boil over medium-high heat. Reduce heat to medium, and simmer until squash is tender when pierced with a fork, about 25 minutes. Remove from heat.

Cook pasta according to package directions, omitting salt and fat; drain well.

Place hot squash mixture in a blender. Add salt, pepper, and Greek yogurt. Blend until smooth.

Place blended squash mixture in a bowl; stir in cheeses. Add pasta to the squash-cheese mixture, stir to combine, and serve immediately.

Yield:

8 servings (approximately 1 cup each)

Nutrition Information (per serving):

379 calories; 12.6 g fat; 32 mg cholesterol; 457 mg sodium; 49.5 g carbohydrate; 5.8 g fiber; 19.6 g protein

Breakfast

Baked Cranberry, Apple, and Walnut Oatmeal

Chocolate Banana Whole-Wheat Waffles

Roasted Poblano and Potato Quiche

Meyer Lemon Ricotta Pancakes

Biscuits and Peppered Sausage Gravy

Stone Fruit Almond Breakfast Crisp

Red Velvet Crepes with Sweet Cream Filling

Bacon and Vegetable Egg Bake

Crock Pot Steel-Cut Oats with Blueberries

Chocolate Glazed Baked Chocolate Donuts

Vegan Banana Nut Muffins

Pumpkin Spice Breakfast Cakes

Goat Cheese, Spinach, and Tomato Quiche

Carrot Cake Pancakes with Cream Cheese Glaze

Baked Cranberry, Apple, and Walnut Oatmeal

3 cups old-fashioned oats
½ cup packed brown sugar
2 teaspoons baking powder
1 teaspoon ground cinnamon
Pinch of nutmeg
¾ teaspoon salt
1 cup skim milk

¼ cup unsalted butter, melted
⅓ cup unsweetened applesauce
2 eggs, beaten
2 medium apples, peeled and diced
⅔ cup cranberries
⅓ cup walnuts

Directions:

Preheat oven to 350°F.

Spray a 9-by-9-inch baking dish with nonstick cooking spray; set aside.

In a large bowl, combine oats, brown sugar, baking powder, cinnamon, nutmeg, and salt, whisking.

In a separate medium-sized bowl, combine milk, butter, applesauce, and eggs. Whisk to combine.

Combine wet ingredients with dry ingredients; incorporate well. Fold in apples, cranberries, and walnuts; spread into the prepared baking dish.

Bake 45 minutes. Allow to cook 5–10 minutes before serving.

Yield:

6 servings

Nutrition Information (per serving):

388 calories; 15.7 g fat; 63 mg cholesterol; 494 mg sodium; 54.2 g carbohydrate; 6.0 g fiber; 9.3 g protein

Shopping Tip:

Old-fashioned oats are less processed than quick-cooking oats. In their most unprocessed form, oats actually look like gravel. Through processing and thinning the oat, we can get it to cook faster and take on different textures. Using quick oats in place of old-fashioned oats sometimes can work, but old-fashioned oats work best in this recipe. I love that baked oatmeal reheats so beautifully. This version is one of my all-time favorites!

Chocolate Banana Whole-Wheat Waffles

1¾ cups whole-wheat pastry flour
¼ teaspoon baking soda
2 teaspoons baking powder
⅛ teaspoon salt
¼ cup unsweetened cocoa powder
2 eggs
1 teaspoon vanilla extract

¾ cup low-fat buttermilk (or milk mixed with
    just less than 1 tablespoon vinegar and
    left to sit 5 minutes)
2 bananas, mashed (about ¾ cup)
2 tablespoons canola oil
1 tablespoon honey

Cook's Comment:

Purchasing unsweetened cocoa powder allows you to add the chocolate into your dishes without any of the guilt. Such as in this recipe, sweeten the chocolate using natural sweeteners, like fruit. Between the banana and honey, this breakfast is not short on sweet chocolate!

Directions:

In a small bowl, combine flour, baking soda, baking powder, sea salt, and cocoa powder. Mix well, and set aside.

In a medium-sized bowl, combine eggs, vanilla, buttermilk, pureed cherries, oil, and honey. Add dry ingredients to wet, and mix well.

Preheat waffle iron or griddle until hot. Use approximately ⅓ cup batter per waffle. Cook according to unit directions, or flip pancakes when bubbles surface and underside is slightly browned, approximately 3 minutes. Flip and cook an additional 1–2 minutes. Serve hot.

Yield:

6 servings (2 waffles or pancakes each)

Nutrition Information (per serving):

259 calories; 7.7 g fat; 63 mg cholesterol; 320 mg sodium;
41.8 g carbohydrate; 6.2 g fiber; 4.0 g protein

Roasted Poblano and Potato Quiche

1 tablespoon extra-virgin olive oil
10 oz. potatoes (about 4 small), diced
¼ onion, diced
4 poblano peppers
5 eggs

¼ cup half-and-half
1 frozen pie crust
½ cup (2 oz.) 2% Mexican-blend cheese, divided
¼ teaspoon salt and pepper, to taste

Directions:

Preheat oven to broil (500°F), and place poblanos on a baking sheet to broil 5–7 minutes, turning once or until charred on all sides; or light a gas burner or grill, and char the skins of the peppers. Place charred peppers in a large plastic zip-top bag to sweat for approximately 10 minutes. Remove charred skins, and discard. Seed and dice peppers; set aside.

Preheat oven to 425°F.

Heat olive oil in a large skillet. Add potatoes, and cook 7–9 minutes or until beginning to brown. Add onion, and cook an additional 5 minutes. Add poblanos and heat through, approximately 2–3 minutes.

Meanwhile, whisk together eggs and half-and-half in a medium-sized bowl. Season with salt and pepper.

Poke the bottom of the pie crust several times with a fork. Sprinkle ¼ cup of cheese on the bottom. Spread potato-poblano mixture into the pie crust. Slowly pour egg mixture over the top, allowing it to flow into the crevices of the quiche. Sprinkle with remaining ¼ cup cheese.

Bake 20–24 minutes or until set. Allow to sit 5–10 minutes before slicing. Serve immediately.

Yield:

6 servings

Nutrition Information (per serving):

288 calories; 15.8 g fat; 163 mg cholesterol; 315 mg sodium; 26.7 g carbohydrate; 1 g fiber; 9.2 g protein

Shopping Tip:

Poblano peppers are milder than a jalapeño and are packed with a unique Mexican flavor. They are one of my favorite ingredients. Before you write off this pepper, know that you can find it in most grocery stores in the produce section for approximately $1.99 per pound.

Meyer Lemon Ricotta Pancakes

4 egg whites
4 egg yolks
12 oz. (1⅓ cups) low-fat ricotta
1½ tablespoons sugar
2 tablespoons Meyer lemon zest, freshly grated
6 oz. (1¼ cups) whole-wheat pastry flour

Directions:

In a mixer or with a hand mixer on medium-high speed, whip egg whites until stiff peaks form. Transfer egg whites to a separate bowl.

In the now-empty mixer bowl, whisk together egg yolks, ricotta, sugar, and lemon zest. Mix in flour, and whisk to combine.

Whisk a small amount of egg whites into yolk-ricotta mixture. Fold in remaining egg whites in 2–3 more sections. Batter will be thick; continue to fold in egg whites until batter is consistent throughout.

Heat a skillet over medium heat; spray with cooking spray, and cook pancakes using the back of a spoon to help spread the batter. You also can cook pancakes on an electric griddle.

Yield:

12 pancakes, about 4 inches each (4 servings, 3 pancakes each)

Nutrition Information (per 3 pancakes):

307 calories; 8.5 g fat; 235 mg cholesterol; 138 mg sodium; 37 g carbohydrate; 3.8 g fiber; 12.8 g protein

Cook's Comment:

Whipping egg whites and folding them into the batter creates fluffy pancakes. With little liquid to the recipe, the pancakes easily can get heavy and dry. Folding is a technique used to create volume in food—be patient, and keep on folding!

Biscuits and Peppered Sausage Gravy

Biscuits:

2 cups all-purpose flour

2 tablespoons granulated sugar

1 tablespoon baking powder

Pinch of salt

⅔ cup milk

⅓ cup unsalted butter, softened

1 tablespoon unsalted butter, melted

Gravy:

10 oz. bulk pork sausage

¼ cup plus 1 tablespoon all-purpose flour

3 cups milk (I used 1%)

1 tablespoon unsalted butter, softened

¼ teaspoon ground black pepper

Pinch of salt

½ teaspoon rosemary, chopped

Cook's Comment:

Rather than starting with a stick of butter and heavy cream, this recipe uses the fat that comes from the ingredients themselves. Pork sausage is high in fat, so there's no need to add more. This recipe doesn't epitomize a nutritious breakfast, but for a splurge, it's ten times better for you than your run-of-the-mill biscuits and gravy, that's for sure!

Directions:
For Biscuits:

Preheat oven to 450°F. Grease a large baking sheet, and set aside.

Place all dry ingredients in a large mixing bowl, and whisk to combine. Stir in milk and softened butter until a crumbly dough forms. Knead until dough is smooth and elastic.

Roll dough out to ½–inch thickness and, using a circle cookie cutter, cut into 12 rounds.

Place rounds on the prepared baking sheet; brush with melted butter, and bake 10–12 minutes. Let cool 5 minutes before serving.

For Gravy:

Heat a large pan over medium-high heat. Add sausage, break it up with a wooden spoon, and cook, stirring occasionally, until well-browned and cooked through, approximately 5 minutes.

Using a slotted spoon, transfer sausage to a bowl, leaving the rendered fat in the skillet. Whisk flour into the fat, and cook, stirring, approximately 1 minute.

While whisking, pour milk and butter into the skillet, and bring gravy to a boil. Lower heat, and simmer gently 2–3 minutes or until desired thickness is reached.

Stir in sausage, and season with pepper, salt, and rosemary. Split biscuits in half, and divide them among plates. Top each biscuit with some gravy, and serve immediately.

Yield:

6 servings (2 biscuits with approximately ⅓ cup gravy)

Nutrition Information (per serving):

498 calories; 27.2 g fat; 60 mg cholesterol; 651 mg sodium; 46 g carbohydrate; 0 g fiber; 16.5 g protein

Stone Fruit Almond Breakfast Crisp

1 cup cherries, stemmed, pitted, and halved

4 ripe nectarines, pitted and chopped

2 ripe plums, pitted and chopped

2 ripe apricots, pitted and chopped

1 tablespoon granulated sugar

2 tablespoons pure maple syrup

1 tablespoon cornstarch

1 teaspoon almond extract

½ teaspoon ground cinnamon

¼ cup almond meal/flour

¼ cup old-fashioned oats

¼ cup (1 oz.) almonds, sliced or chopped

2 tablespoons brown sugar

¼ teaspoon salt

2 tablespoons canola oil

Directions:

Preheat oven to 375°F.

In a large bowl, combine prepared fruit, granulated sugar, maple syrup, cornstarch, almond extract, and ground cinnamon; stir to combine, and set aside.

Stir together almond meal, oats, sliced almonds, raw or brown sugar, and salt in a medium-sized bowl. Drizzle canola oil over mixture, and mix with your fingers until mixture becomes crumbly.

Pour fruit mixture into a lightly greased, 8-inch baking dish. Sprinkle evenly with crisp topping. Bake at 375°F until fruit filling is thick and bubbly, approximately 25–30 minutes.

Let stand at room temperature for approximately 5 minutes before serving.

Yield:

4 servings

Nutrition Information (per serving):

345 calories; 15.3 g fat; 0 mg cholesterol; 179 mg sodium; 51.5 g carbohydrate; 6 g fiber; 6.5 g protein

Cook's Comment:

This can serve as breakfast or dessert. Don't skip the cherries, but do feel free to substitute in the stone fruit of your preference. Peaches are great in this, too! If you love fruit and almonds, this is your match made in heaven!

Red Velvet Crepes with Sweet Cream Filling

Crepes:

2 large eggs

1 large egg yolk

1 cup fat-free milk

½ cup water

Pinch of salt

3 tablespoons unsalted butter, melted

1 teaspoon sugar

Dash of vanilla

2 teaspoons red food coloring

½ cup whole-wheat pastry flour

½ cup all-purpose flour

1½ tablespoons unsweetened cocoa powder

Sweet Cream Cheese Filling:

8 oz. reduced-fat cream cheese, softened

½ teaspoon lemon juice

½ cup powdered sugar

½ cup low-fat ricotta

½ teaspoon vanilla extract

Cook's Comment:

Making crepes takes a hot skillet and a bit of practice. Don't count on your first crepe coming out. Have your batter ready, and swirl the pan quickly. Once you start turning out the crepes, the process will speed up. Regardless, these are worth flying to the moon and back for. Absolutely heavenly!

Directions:

Combine 2 eggs and 1 egg yolk, milk, water, salt, melted butter, sugar, vanilla, and food coloring in a blender, and pulse until foamy. Add flours and cocoa powder, and pulse until smooth. Let batter sit 1 hour.

Prepare filling by mixing all filling ingredients with mixer until well-combined and smooth; set aside.

After batter sits 1 hour, heat a nonstick skillet over medium heat; lightly spray with cooking spray. Pour 1 oz. batter (approximately 3 tablespoons) into the center of the pan, and swirl to spread evenly. Cook until the top loses its gloss, which only should take 1 minute, then flip. Cook the other side approximately 15 seconds, then slide onto a plate.

Repeat with remaining batter.

Prepare crepes by spreading 2 tablespoons cream cheese filling down center of crepe, and roll closed.

Yield:

7 servings (2 crepes with filling each)

Nutrition Information (per serving):

279 calories; 14.6 g fat; 120 mg cholesterol; 190 mg sodium; 26.4 g carbohydrate; 1.3 g fiber; 8 g protein

Bacon and Vegetable Egg Bake

Olive oil cooking spray

2 teaspoons olive oil

½ yellow onion, diced

⅛ teaspoon salt and pepper

1 large green bell pepper, diced

½ cup carrot, shredded

5 slices nitrate-free bacon

10 large eggs

1 cup nonfat milk

½ teaspoon salt and pepper

1 cup 2% Colby Jack cheese, shredded

1 cup spinach, loosely packed

Directions:

Preheat oven to 350°F.

Spray a 9-by-13-inch glass dish with olive oil spray; set aside.

Heat oil in a medium-sized skillet. Add onions and ⅛ teaspoon salt and pepper, and sauté 2–3 minutes until softened. Add bell pepper and carrot. Sauté an additional 3–4 minutes; layer vegetables in the bottom of the 9-by-13-inch dish.

In the same skillet, add bacon slices, and cook until crisp. Remove, and set on a paper towel to drain excess grease.

Meanwhile, whisk together eggs and milk in a large bowl. Add ½ teaspoon salt, cheese, and spinach. Pour eggs over vegetables, and gently press spinach into egg mixture. Crumble bacon using your fingers over the top of the eggs. Bake 30 minutes.

Yield:

8 servings

Nutrition Information (per serving):

184 calories; 12.6 g fat; 247 mg cholesterol; 531 mg sodium; 4.3 g carbohydrate; 0.8 g fiber; 14.0 g protein

Shopping Tip:

Using "uncured" bacon is the best way to avoid sodium nitrate. Nitrates are linked to colon and rectal cancers, and their only purpose is to prevent rancidity and keep meat pink—*bleck!*

Crock Pot Steel-Cut Oats with Blueberries

1 cup steel-cut oats
4 cups unsweetened coconut milk
¼ cup turbinado

1 teaspoon vanilla
2 cups blueberries

Directions:

Use a slow-cooker liner for easy cleanup.

Combine ingredients in the slow cooker; cover, and cook on low 8–9 hours. Stir before serving.

Yield:

4 servings (approximately 1 cup each)

Nutrition Information (per serving):

302 calories; 7.5 g fat; 0 mg cholesterol; 16 mg sodium; 53.5 g carbohydrate; 8.0 g fiber; 7.5 g protein

Nutrition Note:

Carbohydrates get such a bad reputation, and I hate that! Meals like this are packed with nutrition—tons of fiber and antioxidants. Don't forget to consider balance in terms of the day; a meal that is higher in carbohydrates is perfectly healthful. The body looks at averages—the days and weeks as a whole, not single meals. Always be sure to look at the whole picture, and remember, adults require a *minimum* of 130 g carbohydrates per day for proper bodily function . . . and that includes diabetics!

Remember:

A carbohydrate-controlled diet is optimal for diabetics.

Chocolate Glazed Baked Chocolate Donuts

Donuts:

1 cup whole-wheat pastry flour

¼ cup unsweetened cocoa powder

¼ cup sugar

1 tablespoon baking powder

¼ teaspoon salt

1 egg

½ cup unsweetened almond milk

1 teaspoon vanilla

1 tablespoon canola oil

3 tablespoons unsweetened applesauce

Chocolate Glaze:

½ cup semisweet chocolate chips

1 teaspoon canola oil

1 tablespoon corn syrup

¼ teaspoon vanilla extract

Directions:

Preheat oven to 450°F, and coat a donut pan liberally with cooking spray.

Stir together flour, cocoa powder, sugar, baking powder, and salt in a large bowl. Add egg, milk, vanilla, oil, and applesauce; stir 1 minute.

Fill each cavity in the pan halfway with batter. Bake 7–8 minutes or until donuts spring back when lightly touched. Cool completely.

Meanwhile, melt chocolate in a microwave-safe bowl. Add corn syrup and oil, and microwave in 20-second increments, stirring in-between. Stir in vanilla. Dunk each donut into the glaze, and allow to set.

Yield:

14 donuts

Nutrition Information (per donut):

93 calories; 3.4 g fat; 15 mg cholesterol; 157 mg sodium; 15.2 g carbohydrate; 1.9 g fiber; 1.1 g protein

Nutrition Note:

Making your favorite treats at home gives you the chance to control what goes into your food. Most donuts contain much more than 200–300 calories per piece . . . not to mention dozens of grams of fat! I can make donuts at home that have less than half the number of calories and one-third less fat! Plus, they still taste great!

Vegan Banana Nut Muffins

3 large ripe bananas
¼ cup canola oil
1 teaspoon vanilla
⅓ cup turbinado
⅓ cup brown sugar
2 cups whole-wheat pastry flour

1 teaspoon salt
1 teaspoon baking soda
1 tablespoon cinnamon
1 teaspoon ground nutmeg
½ teaspoon ground ginger
½ cup walnuts, chopped

Directions:

Preheat oven to 350°F. Line a muffin tin.

In a medium-sized bowl using a fork, mash banana against the sides of the bowl. Stir or whisk in oil, vanilla, and sugar.

In a separate bowl, whisk together flour, salt, baking soda, and spices.

Add wet ingredients to dry ingredients, and stir until combined. Then, fold in walnuts. Pour into each muffin well until nearly full. Bake 25 minutes.

Yield:

12 large muffins

Nutrition Information (per muffin):

210 calories; 7.9 g fat; 0 mg cholesterol; 292 mg sodium; 33.5 g carbohydrate; 3.2 g fiber; 1.2 g protein

Nutrition Note:

Turbinado is a 100% cane sugar that retains molasses flavor and a beautiful brown color. Turbinado is coarse and has large crystals, yet can be substituted in most any recipe for granulated sugar. I love the flavor!

Pumpkin Spice Breakfast Cakes

¼ cup unsalted butter, softened

¼ cup nonfat plain Greek yogurt

¼ cup sugar

2 eggs

1 teaspoon vanilla

¾ cup canned pumpkin

1 cup whole-wheat pastry flour

1 teaspoon baking powder

¼ teaspoon salt

½ teaspoon pumpkin pie spice

½ teaspoon cinnamon

Directions:

Preheat oven to 350°F. Spray 4 ramekins with cooking spray, and arrange on a lined baking sheet.

In a medium-sized bowl, cream together butter, yogurt, and sugar. Whisk in eggs, vanilla, and pumpkin. Combine well.

In a small bowl, whisk together flour, baking powder, salt, and spices. Add wet ingredients to dry ingredients, and mix until just combined.

Fill each ramekin ¾ full, and bake 30–35 minutes or until an inserted toothpick comes out clean. Allow to cool 5–10 minutes before serving warm.

Yield:

4 servings

Nutrition Information (per serving):

313 calories; 14.3 g fat; 93 mg cholesterol; 306 mg sodium; 38.0 g carbohydrate; 5.0 g fiber; 5.3 g protein

Nutrition Note:

Cooking in ramekins is the perfect brain tease. You get to eat the whole portion, so you don't feel deprived, yet the ramekins are perfect portions. I have made these every fall for several years and changed the recipe every time. This one, though. . . . It's the winner. Enjoy!

Goat Cheese, Spinach, and Tomato Quiche

1 large russet potato, sliced into very thin
    rounds
8 large eggs
¼ cup skim milk
1 teaspoon Italian seasoning

¾ teaspoon salt
½ teaspoon pepper
1 Roma tomato, sliced
2 cups fresh baby spinach, tightly packed
3 oz. goat cheese

Directions:

Preheat oven to 375°F.

Spray a 9-inch pie plate with nonstick spray. Layer potato rounds on the bottom and sides of the pan in a single layer. With remaining potato rounds, cover any holes in the potato layer (if you don't cover all the holes, don't worry). Bake potatoes in the oven for approximately 15 minutes.

Meanwhile, in a large bowl, whisk together eggs and milk until smooth. Add seasonings, and whisk until well-combined. When potatoes are done par-baking, layer spinach on top of potatoes and goat cheese on top of spinach in small chunks. Gently pour egg mixture over the top. Layer tomatoes on top of egg mixture. Bake at 375°F 30–40 minutes.

If desired, broil quiche 1–2 minutes to brown the top slightly. Remove from oven, and let sit 5 minutes before serving.

Yield:

8 slices (⅛ of 9-inch quiche per serving)

Nutrition Information (per serving):

124 calories; 6.9 g fat; 221 mg cholesterol; 327 mg sodium; 6.5 g carbohydrate; 0.9 g fiber; 8.8 g protein

Nutrition Note:

Sliced potatoes make for a wonderful quiche crust—just be sure to cut them nice and thin! By using potatoes in place of a traditional crust, you drastically cut down on the amount of fat in the recipe; plus, you're adding fiber, vitamins, and minerals. I'm all for sneaking in vegetables for breakfast or brunch!

Carrot Cake Pancakes with Cream Cheese Glaze

Pancakes:

2¼ cups whole-wheat pastry flour

¼ cup brown sugar

2 teaspoons cinnamon

2¼ teaspoons baking powder

¾ teaspoons baking soda

½ teaspoon salt

1½ cups low-fat buttermilk

3 eggs, lightly beaten

1½ tablespoons canola oil

1½ teaspoons vanilla extract

3 cups carrots, peeled and shredded (about 2 lbs)

⅓ cup walnuts, chopped

Glaze:

4 oz. ⅓ less fat cream cheese, at room temperature

¼ cup powdered sugar

1 teaspoon vanilla extract

3 tablespoons skim milk; add more, if needed to thin

Nutrition Note:

Between the whole-wheat pastry flour and carrots, this breakfast is packed with fiber. It's also packed with flavor. I assure you, this recipe will make you think twice. You may ask yourself, "Can eating healthy really taste this good?" Yes . . . yes, it can!

Directions:

In a medium-sized bowl, whisk flour, sugar, cinnamon, baking powder, baking soda, and salt. Set aside.

In a large bowl, whisk together buttermilk, eggs, oil, and vanilla until combined.

Add dry ingredients to wet ingredients, gently stir until blended. Fold in carrots and walnuts. Let batter sit 10 minutes.

Microwave cream cheese approximately 15–20 seconds to soften. Whisk remaining ingredients for the glaze, adding additional milk, if needed, to thin.

Meanwhile, preheat large nonstick skillet or griddle to medium.

Pour batter onto griddle using a ¼ measuring cup, spreading batter with the flat bottom. Flip pancakes when tops are covered with bubbles and edges look cooked (approximately 2–3 minutes). Cook the other side until set (approximately 2 minutes). Serve warm with cream cheese glaze.

Yield:

7 servings (2 pancakes each with about 1½ tablespoons glaze)

Nutrition Information (per serving):

365 calories; 12.9 g fat; 93 mg cholesterol; 644 mg sodium; 50.6 g carbohydrate; 6.4 g fiber; 7.9 g protein

Finish It Off, Hold the Guilt

Mini Honey Cheesecakes with Raspberry Swirl

Lightened-Up Apple Crisp

Greek Yogurt Ice Cream

Chocolate Dutch Baby

Best Butter-less Chocolate Chip Cookies

Sugar-Free Chocolate Coconut Almond Cups

Watermelon Slush

Cherry Avocado Pops

Mini Honey Cheesecakes with Raspberry Swirl

Crust:
½ cup walnuts
½ cup whole-wheat pastry flour
Pinch of salt
2 tablespoons unsalted butter
1 tablespoon honey

Topping:
1 pint (6 oz.) fresh or frozen raspberries
1 tablespoon honey

Filling:
1 cup low-fat ricotta
8 oz. reduced-fat cream cheese, at room
  temperature
¼ cup sugar
2 tablespoons honey
1 teaspoon lemon juice
½ teaspoon vanilla
2 eggs, at room temperature

Nutrition Note:

Making "mini" treats and snacks is ideal for portion control. For high-calorie dessert items like cheesecake, this recipe not only is lightened up, but also keeps the portion in check.

Directions:

Preheat oven to 325°F, and line a muffin tin with 12 muffin liners.

To prepare crust, combine nuts, flour, and salt in the bowl of a food processor, and process until finely ground. Add butter and honey; pulse to a coarse crumb. Gently press 2 teaspoons crust mixture into each cupcake liner using fingertips. Bake 10–12 minutes, until slightly golden brown. Remove from oven, and set aside to cool.

In a blender or food processor, combine raspberries and honey; blend until smooth. Pour through a fine mesh strainer to remove seeds and reserve raspberry juice.

Using a stand or hand mixer, beat cream cheese until smooth; add ricotta, and mix to combine. Mix in remaining filling ingredients until incorporated well.

Fill each cupcake well with filling. Top filling with a few dots of raspberry puree, and swirl with a toothpick to create a marbled effect.

Bake 23–28 minutes, until filling is puffed and mostly set. Allow cheesecakes to cool completely, then refrigerate for at least 4 hours before serving.

Yield:

12 mini cheesecakes

Nutrition Information (per cheesecake):

181 calories; 10.3 g fat; 49 mg cholesterol; 110 mg sodium; 16.8 g carbohydrate; 1.4 g fiber; 4.8 g protein

Lightened-Up Apple Crisp

4 apples, peeled, cored, and diced

2 tablespoons sugar

2 teaspoons cornstarch

Juice of ½ lemon

1 tablespoon cinnamon

1 cup old-fashioned rolled oats

¼ cup whole-wheat pastry flour

⅓ cup brown sugar

¼ cup (½ stick) cold unsalted butter, cut into pieces

Directions:

Preheat oven to 375°F.

Place apples in baking dish. Sprinkle apples with 2 tablespoons granulated sugar, cornstarch, lemon juice, and cinnamon; toss to combine.

In a medium-sized bowl, combine oats, flour, and sugar. Cut in butter using a pastry blender, forks, or your fingers until it resembles coarse crumbs. Top apples evenly with crumble mixture.

Bake approximately 25–30 minutes until filling is bubbly and topping is lightly browned. Cool approximately 5–10 minutes before serving.

Yield:

7 servings (about ⅔ cup each)

Nutrition Information (per serving):

212 calories; 7.3 g fat; 0 mg cholesterol; 54 mg sodium; 36.9 g carbohydrate; 4.4 g fiber; 1.4 g protein

Cook's Comment:

Fruit is naturally sweet and offers up nutritional perks such as fiber, vitamins, and minerals. Buying in-season fruit means you not only buy what's best, but you also can keep costs down.

Use gluten-free flour for a gluten-friendly dessert.

Greek Yogurt Ice Cream

1 cup half-and-half
1 cup whole milk
¾ cup sugar, divided
3 large egg yolks

1 cup 2% Greek-style yogurt
Pinch of salt
1 vanilla bean, with seeds removed (optional)

Fun Fact:

Plain Greek yogurt is suitable for everything from breakfast parfaits to a replacement for sour cream and even ice cream-making. This readily available ingredient is high in protein and offers up probiotics. It's also low in fat and has a unique, tangy flavor that so many people are discovering they love!

Directions:

Combine half-and-half, whole milk, and ½ cup sugar in heavy medium-sized saucepan. Bring mixture to a simmer, dissolving sugar. Whisk 3 large egg yolks and remaining ¼ cup sugar in large heat-proof bowl until blended. Gradually add hot cream mixture to yolk mixture, and whisk until blended.

Return mixture to saucepan, and stir over medium-low heat until custard thickens slightly and coats back of spoon or when instant-read thermometer registers 170°F, about 3 minutes (do not boil).

Pour custard through strainer set over medium-sized bowl. Place bowl with custard in larger bowl filled halfway with ice water. Whisk occasionally until custard is almost cool to touch, about 5 minutes. Remove bowl with custard from ice water. Whisk yogurt and pinch of salt into custard. Refrigerate custard until well-chilled.

Transfer custard to ice cream maker, and process according to manufacturer's instructions. Transfer yogurt ice cream to freezer container; freeze until firm before serving.

Yield:

3½ cups (7 servings; ½ cup each)

Nutrition Information (per serving):

188 calories; 7.3 g fat; 110 mg cholesterol; 81 mg sodium; 24.9 g carbohydrate; 0 g fiber; 5.6 g protein

Chocolate Dutch Baby

¾ cup 2% milk

3 large eggs

½ cup whole-wheat pastry flour

¼ cup unsweetened cocoa powder

¼ teaspoon sea salt

½ teaspoon vanilla

¼ cup sugar

2 tablespoons unsalted butter

Powdered sugar, for dusting

Cook's Comment:

Dutch babies are simple to whip together, and you can't help but be floored by the low-calorie count and carbohydrate content, which comes in at fewer than 15 g per serving! You'll feel like you're having dessert in the middle of Europe with one of these around. I promise!

Directions:

Place a 10-inch cast-iron skillet in the oven, and preheat to 425°F (or prepare a pie dish by buttering with 2 tablespoons butter).

To prepare batter, whisk everything together, being sure to sift cocoa powder to eliminate lumps.

Once well-mixed and when the oven is hot, add butter to the hot cast-iron skillet, and swirl around to melt and coat the pan. Once melted, pour batter, and place into oven. Bake 20 minutes or until the Dutch baby is puffed up around the edges and completely set in the middle. When done, remove from oven, and cool approximately 5 minutes. Dust with powdered sugar.

Yield:

8 slices (⅛ of a 10-inch "pie")

Nutrition Information (per slice):

118 calories; 5.4 g fat; 83 mg cholesterol; 108 mg sodium; 14.4 g carbohydrate; 1.8 g fiber; 3.4 g protein

Best Butter-less Chocolate Chip Cookies

½ cup coconut oil, melted

1 cup plus 1 tablespoon brown sugar, packed

2 large eggs, at room temperature

1 tablespoon pure vanilla extract

1¾ cups whole-wheat pastry flour

½ teaspoon salt

1 teaspoon baking powder

¼ teaspoon baking soda

10 oz. semisweet chocolate chips

Directions:

Preheat oven to 375°F. Line baking sheets with parchment paper or silicone pad.

In a large bowl, beat together coconut oil and brown sugar with mixer. Add in eggs, and beat until fluffy. Add vanilla extract.

In medium-sized bowl, combine flour, baking soda, salt, and baking powder with whisk. Mix flour mixture into coconut-oil mixture with a wooden spoon until all flour is incorporated. Add chocolate chips, and mix well.

Drop mixture with rounded tablespoons onto prepared baking sheets. Bake approximately 8–10 minutes or until slightly brown around the edges. Let rest on cookie sheet for a few minutes before moving to rack to cool completely.

Yield:

40 cookies

Nutrition Information (per cookie):

96 calories; 4.9 g fat; 9 mg cholesterol; 70 mg sodium; 13 g carbohydrate; 1 g fiber; 0.8 g protein

Nutrition Note:

Coconut oil is a tropical oil that is high in saturated fat, but packed with delicious coconut flavor, making it ideal for desserts and stir frys. Due to the nature of the coconut oil chemical structure, it is absorbed differently in the body. Research is currently looking into its "ranking" among other fats. This recipe simply uses coconut oil in place of butter. So much flavor!

Sugar-Free Chocolate Coconut Almonds Cups

¼ cup coconut oil

½ cup almond butter

1½ teaspoons pure vanilla extract

¼ cup unsweetened cocoa powder

3 packets stevia

2 tablespoons unsweetened coconut, shredded

14 unsalted almonds

Directions:

Line a mini-muffin tray with 14 paper liners.

In a microwave-safe bowl, melt coconut oil in the microwave, about 45–60 seconds. Stir in almond butter, vanilla, cocoa, stevia, and coconut. Distribute mixture among the 14 wells, filling until nearly full.

Freeze cups 8–10 minutes; remove, and gently press an almond into each cup. Freeze until ready to consume.

Yield:

14 cups

Nutrition Information (per cup):

104 calories; 10.4 g fat; 0 mg cholesterol; 6 mg sodium; 3.0 g carbohydrate; 1.7 g fiber; 2.8 g protein

Nutrition Note:

This is the only sugar-free dessert I've made successfully. Feel free to substitute your calorie-free sweetener of choice. Almond Joys were the inspiration for this healthful rendition. It's perfect for diabetics or those who hate to cook but love coconut.

Watermelon Slush

4 cups watermelon, diced and frozen

2 limes, juiced

2 tablespoons honey

¾–1 cup water

Directions:

Blend all ingredients in a blender until smooth. Serve immediately.

Yield:

4 servings (1 cup each)

Nutrition Information (per serving):

82 calories; 0 g fat; 0 mg cholesterol; 3 mg sodium; 21.5 g carbohydrate; 1 g fiber; 1 g protein

Fun Fact:

I love to buy fruit, and lots of it, when it's in season. I freeze whatever I don't eat within a week or so and can enjoy fruit at its peak ripeness all year-round. This recipe is perfect for a hot summer day. The hint of honey is my favorite touch!

Cherry Avocado Pops

2 cups cherries, fresh or frozen, pitted

1 avocado

1 cup unsweetened coconut milk

2 tablespoons honey

Directions:

Combine all ingredients in a blender or food processor, and process until smooth. Pour evenly into 9 (3 oz.) popsicle wells, and freeze 4 hours or longer to harden.

Remove pops from freezer 10 minutes before serving to loosen from the wells.

Yield:

9 (3 oz.) pops

Nutrition Information (per pop):

71 calories; 3.7 g fat; 0 mg cholesterol; 3 mg sodium; 11 g carbohydrate; 1.9 g fiber; 0.6 g protein

Fun Fact:

You can make popsicles out of . . . anything! This recipe uses one of my favorite fruits (substitute in whatever you love most), along with heart-healthy avocado. The avocado not only adds nutrition, but also a creamy texture.

METRIC AND IMPERIAL CONVERSIONS

(These conversions are rounded for convenience)

Ingredient	Cups/Tablespoons/ Teaspoons	Ounces	Grams/Milliliters
Butter	1 cup=16 tablespoons= 2 sticks	8 ounces	230 grams
Cream cheese	1 tablespoon	0.5 ounce	14.5 grams
Cheese, shredded	1 cup	4 ounces	110 grams
Cornstarch	1 tablespoon	0.3 ounce	8 grams
Flour, all-purpose	1 cup/1 tablespoon	4.5 ounces/0.3 ounce	125 grams/8 grams
Flour, whole wheat	1 cup	4 ounces	120 grams
Fruit, dried	1 cup	4 ounces	120 grams
Fruits or veggies, chopped	1 cup	5 to 7 ounces	145 to 200 grams
Fruits or veggies, pureed	1 cup	8.5 ounces	245 grams
Honey, maple syrup, or corn syrup	1 tablespoon	.75 ounce	20 grams
Liquids: cream, milk, water, or juice	1 cup	8 fluid ounces	240 ml
Oats	1 cup	5.5 ounces	150 grams
Salt	1 teaspoon	0.2 ounces	6 grams
Spices: cinnamon, cloves, ginger, or nutmeg (ground)	1 teaspoon	0.2 ounce	5 ml
Sugar, brown, firmly packed	1 cup	7 ounces	200 grams
Sugar, white	1 cup/1 tablespoon	7 ounces/0.5 ounce	200 grams/12.5 grams
Vanilla extract	1 teaspoon	0.2 ounce	4 grams

OVEN TEMPERATURES

Fahrenheit	Celcius	Gas Mark
225°	110°	¼
250°	120°	½
275°	140°	1
300°	150°	2
325°	160°	3
350°	180°	4
375°	190°	5
400°	200°	6
425°	220°	7
450°	230°	8